Simplicity's

QUICK & EASY SEWING FOR THE HOME

TABLE TOPPERS

Simplicity's

QUICK & EASY SEWING FOR THE HOME
TABLE TOPPERS

EDITED BY ANNE MARIE SOTO

AND THE

STAFF OF THE SIMPLICITY PATTERN COMPANY

Rodale Press, Inc.
Emmaus, Pennsylvania

OUR MISSION

We publish books that empower people's lives.

RODALE BOOKS

SIMPLICITY

Editor: Anne Marie Soto
Contributing Editor: Janis Bullis
Cover and Interior Designer: Christine Swirnoff
Art Direction and Production: Ripinsky & Company
Administrative Manager: Cheryl Dick
Senior Illustrator: Phoebe Gaughan
Illustrator: Deborah Sottile
Copy Editor: Didi Charney
Senior Vice President, Product, Simplicity Patterns: Judy Raymond

RODALE BOOKS

Editor: Susan Weaver
Designer: Patricia Field
Copy Editor: Carolyn Mandarano
Manufacturing Coordinator: Jodi Schaffer
Senior Editor, Craft Books: Cheryl Winters-Tetreau
Editorial Director, Home and Garden: Margaret Lydic Balitas
Editor-in-Chief: William Gottlieb

On the cover: Quick Patch, page 93

If you have any questions or comments concerning this book, please write to:

Rodale Press, Inc.
Book Readers' Service
33 East Minor Street
Emmaus, PA 18098

Library of Congress Cataloging-in-Publication Data

Simplicity's quick and easy sewing for the home. Table toppers / edited by Anne Marie Soto
and the staff of the Simplicity Pattern Company.
        p.   cm.
ISBN 0–87596–677–2 hardcover
1. Household linens. 2. Table setting and decoration. 3. Machine sewing.
I. Soto, Anne Marie. II. Simplicity Pattern Co.
TT387.S549 1995
646.2'1—dc20   95–16404

Distributed in the book trade by St. Martin's Press

2 4 6 8 10 9 7 5 3 1 hardcover

CONTENTS

INTRODUCTION

When is a table not just a table? When it meets up with a little fabric magic!

We at Simplicity have learned that even the "sometime . . . maybe" crowd of would-be sewers and crafters is intrigued by tabletop projects. After all, what could be easier to make than something that is basically a flat piece of fabric, with nary a dart, collar, or buttonhole in sight! And in addition to being easy to sew, tablecloths, place mats, and napkins are the perfect canvases for exploring some fabulous embellishment techniques.

In the pages of this book, you'll learn how to work your own fabric magic with more than 30 different projects. Transform an inexpensive table into a decorative showpiece. Make an everyday meal a festive occasion. Create beautiful place mats, napkins, and fabric-based napkin rings. Refurbish careworn dining chairs and kitchen stools with coordinating cushions and covers.

For easy reference, the book is divided into three parts. "Round About" features floor-length, layered table coverings that are perfect for bedroom or living room, foyer or den. By providing fashionable camouflages for old wood or inexpensive cardboard tables, these fabric coverings can convert something that's strictly utilitarian into an item of beauty—one with new-found storage space beneath its generous skirts!

For a collection of exciting variations on the basic rectangular cloth, there's "Cover Me Pretty." This section shows what can be done with fabric painting and stenciling techniques, appliqué details, and a fresh perspective on proportions.

"Place Settings" includes ten different place mats, plus chair and stool covers, napkins, napkin rings, and table runners. There's even a special collection of super-easy Christmas projects. Pieced, appliquéd, and folded patchwork embellishments provide visual excitement.

Each project is introduced with a full-page, four-color photograph and is followed by complete, self-contained instructions, including a supply list with fabric suggestions and yardage requirements, cutting directions, sewing directions, and embellishment information.

"Sew Simple" tips, scattered throughout the book, contain information on tools and techniques for achieving professional results with minimal effort. Some of these tips focus on a specific project; others will help you sew faster and easier, regardless of the project.

"Design Plus" tips focus on ways to maximize the design potential of a specific project by simply changing the fabric, the color, or the trim. In this series, we also share some general tips from professional interior designers for planning the best possible decor.

"Terms & Techniques" at the back of this book contains additional helpful information. Here's where you'll learn how to customize the tablecloth directions for any size table. Stitching terms, general stenciling directions, and machine appliqué techniques, plus instructions on how to cut bias strips, apply bias binding, and create custom piping, are all included in this helpful section. When your selected project utilizes any of these techniques, the instructions will refer you directly to the appropriate "Terms & Techniques" page.

So whether your goal is to enhance your own decor, make a memorable gift, or explore a new embellishment technique, you're sure to find what you seek in the pages of this book.

Simplicity Pattern Company

ROUND ABOUT

Dressed in coordinating fabrics,
this space-saving half-round table makes a bold
statement in a small room or hallway.

BASIC BEAUTY

Size:

To fit a 20″ (51cm) diameter × 28¾″ (73cm) high half-round decorator table

SUPPLIES

- *3¼ yards (3m) of 45″ (115cm) wide decorator fabric, such as chintz, calico, or broadcloth**
- *1 yard (1m) of 45″ (115cm) wide contrasting decorator fabric*
- *½ yard (0.5m) of 45″ (115cm) wide polyester batting*
- *Brown paper*
- *Tape measure*
- *One 36″ (91.5cm) straight-edge ruler*
- *Dressmaker's chalk or a soft lead pencil*

*See "Sew Simple" on page 12 for additional information.

CUTTING DIRECTIONS

All measurements include ½″ (1.3cm) seam allowances.

Make the tabletop pattern by tracing the top of the half-round table onto the brown paper. Add ½″ (1.3cm) all around, as shown in **Diagram 1.**

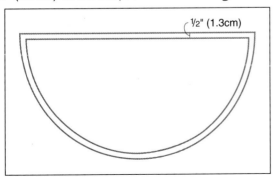

½″ (1.3cm)

Diagram 1

From the decorator fabric, cut:

- *1 top, using the paper pattern*
- *Two 30″ × 45″ (76cm × 115cm) front panels, using the full width of the fabric for each panel. Split one panel in half lengthwise and cut two 30″ (76cm) long front side panels.*

Fold the remaining decorator fabric in half so that the selvage edges match. Referring to **Diagram 2,** fold the paper pattern in half crosswise. Match the folded edge of the pattern to the folded edge of the fabric. Measure from the outside corner of the paper pattern to the diagonally opposite outside corner of the fabric. Shift the paper pattern up or down until this diagonal measurement is 30″ (76cm). Use the chalk or pencil to draw the diagonal line and a line along the straight edge of the paper pattern. Draw another line across the fabric to intersect with the bottom of the diagonal line. Cut out the skirt back along these marked lines.

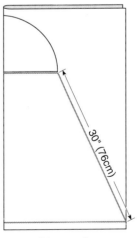

30″ (76cm)

Diagram 2

From the contrasting decorator fabric, cut one 36″ (91.5cm) square tablecloth.

From the batting and using the brown paper pattern, cut one top batting.

SEWING DIRECTIONS

1 Preparing the top

With cut edges matching, pin the top batting to the wrong side of the top. Referring to **Diagram 3,** machine baste ⅜″ (1cm) from the edges. Measure along the curved edge and use the chalk or pencil to mark 11″ (28cm) from one back corner. Repeat, marking 11″ (28cm) from the other back corner.

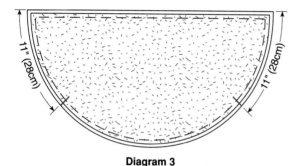

Diagram 3

🧵 SEW SIMPLE

Although the average half-round decorator table is 28¾″ (73cm) high, your table may be taller or shorter. Measure your table from the top outer edge to the floor and then add 1¼″ (3.2cm). Substitute this new measurement wherever the measurement 30″ (76cm) appears in these directions.

2 Preparing the skirt

With right sides together, stitch one front side panel to each side edge of the front center panel, as shown in **Diagram 4.** Press the seams open. Machine baste along one long edge of the skirt front, ¼″ (6mm) and ¾″ (2cm) from the edge, leaving long thread tails at the beginning and end of each row of stitches. Begin and end the basting stitches ½″ (1.3cm) from the side edges.

With right sides together, stitch the skirt front to the skirt back along the side edges. Press the seams open.

3 Hemming the skirt

Referring to **Diagram 5,** press under ½″ (1.3cm) on the long edge without the basting. Tuck the raw edge in to meet the crease. Press again. Stitch close to the second fold.

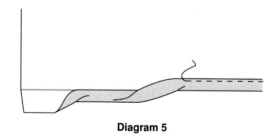

Diagram 5

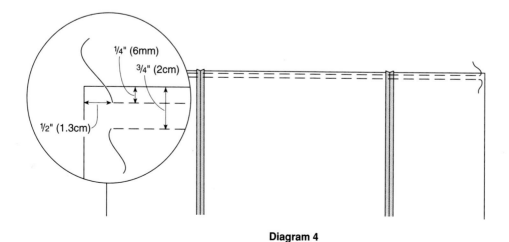

¼" (6mm)

¾" (2cm)

½" (1.3cm)

Diagram 4

4 Attaching the skirt

With right sides together, pin the skirt to the top, matching the two front seams to the 11″ (28cm) markings and the side seams to the corners. Pull up the basting stitches, gathering the skirt front until the fullness is evenly distributed. Stitch the skirt back to the top, beginning and ending the stitching ½″ (1.3cm) from the corners, as shown in **Diagram 6.** Stitch the skirt front to the top, beginning and ending the stitching ½″ (1.3cm) from the corners.

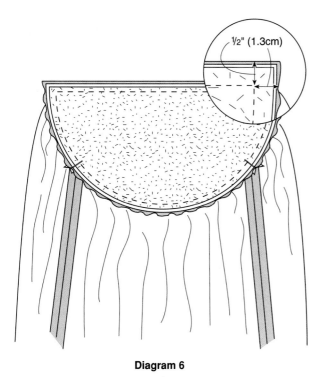

Diagram 6

Turn the skirt right side out.

5 Hemming the tablecloth

Referring to **Diagram 7,** press under ½″ (1.3cm) on two opposite edges of the 36″ (91.5cm) square tablecloth. Tuck each raw edge in to meet the crease. Press again. Stitch close to the second fold. Repeat for the remaining opposite edges.

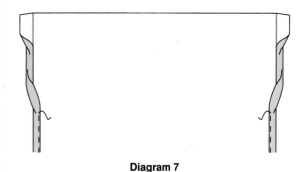

Diagram 7

INSTALLATION

Cover the half-round table with the skirt. Cover the top of the table with the tablecloth, as shown in the photograph on page 10.

⊕ DESIGN PLUS

A wall-mounted shelf is an easy-to-make substitute for a half-round decorator table. Cut a piece of wood into the desired size half-circle. Mount it 28¾″ (73cm) from the floor, using angle brackets and leaving a ¼″ (6mm) space between the wall and the wood. Cut two slits in the back of the skirt to accommodate the brackets.

You don't need to fuss to make an attractive tablecloth. Fashion a real beauty with little more than coordinating sheets and 2-cord shirring tape.

PETTICOAT SKIRT

Size:

To fit a 20″ (51cm) diameter × 25″ (63.5cm) high decorator table

To adjust these directions for a different size table, review the information on page 123 for customizing a tablecloth.

SUPPLIES

- *1 flat full-size striped sheet**
- *1 flat full-size solid sheet**
- *1⅝ yards (1.5m) of 2-cord shirring tape*
- *Tape measure*
- *Water-soluble marking pen*
- *Dressmaker's chalk*
- *Liquid fray preventer*

*The underskirt and overskirt can also be made from 45″ (115cm) wide fabric. See "Design Plus" for additional information.

CUTTING DIRECTIONS

All measurements include ½″ (1.3cm) seam allowances.

From the striped sheet, cut:

- *One 21″ (53.5cm) square underskirt top*
- *Two 21″ × 80″ (53.5cm × 204cm) underskirt side sections*

From the solid sheet, cut:

- *One 31″ (78.5cm) square overskirt top*
- *Four 6″ × 80″ (15cm × 204cm) underskirt ruffle sections*
- *Two 2½″ × 65″ (6.3cm × 165cm) overskirt ruffle sections*

✦ DESIGN PLUS

To make this table topper from fabric instead of sheets, purchase 3 yards (2.8m) of 45″ (115cm) wide decorator fabric and 2½ yards (2.3m) of 45″ (115cm) wide contrasting decorator fabric.

From the decorator fabric, cut:

- *One 21″ (53.5cm) square underskirt top*
- *Four 21″ × 45″ (53.5cm × 115cm) underskirt side sections*

From the contrasting decorator fabric, cut:

- *One 31″ (78.5cm) square overskirt top*
- *Eight 6″ × 45″ (15cm × 115cm) underskirt ruffle sections*
- *Three 2½″ × 45″ (6.3cm × 115cm) overskirt ruffle sections*

SEWING DIRECTIONS

1 Assembling the underskirt

Fold the 21″ (53.5cm) square underskirt top in half and then in quarters, matching the cut edges. Pin the layers together at the cut edges. Using the tape measure and marking pen, measure and mark a quarter-circle with a 10½″ (26.5cm) radius, as shown in **Diagram 1**. Cut along the marked line, through all of the layers. Remove the pins and unfold the underskirt top.

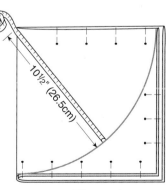

Diagram 1

Referring to **Diagram 2,** with right sides together, stitch the underskirt side sections together at the ends to form one continuous skirt. Press the seams open. Machine baste along one long edge, following the directions on page 124 for preparing a ruffle.

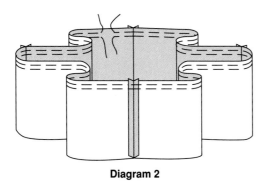

Diagram 2

Divide and mark the upper and lower edges of the underskirt side into eight equal parts.

Divide and mark the edge of the underskirt top into eight equal parts, as shown in **Diagram 3.**

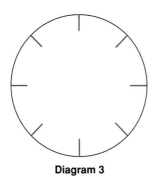

Diagram 3

Referring to **Diagram 4,** with right sides together, stitch the underskirt side to the underskirt top, following the directions on page 124 for gathering and attaching a ruffle.

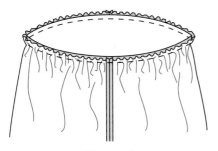

Diagram 4

2 Trimming the underskirt

Referring to **Diagram 5,** with right sides together, stitch the underskirt ruffle sections together at the ends to form one continuous ruffle. Press the seams open. Press under ½″ (1.3cm) on one long edge. Tuck the raw edge in to meet the crease. Press again. Stitch close to the second fold. Machine baste along the raw edge, following the directions on page 124 for preparing a ruffle.

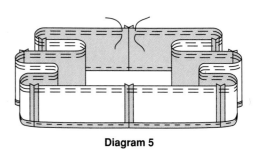

Diagram 5

Divide and mark the underskirt ruffle into eight equal parts.

Referring to **Diagram 6,** with right sides together, stitch the underskirt ruffle to the lower edge of the underskirt side, following the directions on page 124 for gathering and attaching a ruffle. Press the seam allowances toward the underskirt side.

Diagram 6

3 Assembling the overskirt

Fold the 31″ (78.5cm) square overskirt top in half and then in quarters, matching the cut edges. Pin the layers together at the cut edges. Using the tape measure and marking pen, measure and mark a quarter-circle with a 15½″ (39.5cm) radius, as shown in **Diagram 7.** Cut along the marked line, through all of the layers. Remove the pins and unfold the overskirt top.

Referring to **Diagram 8,** with right sides together, fold the overskirt top in half, then in quarters, and then in eighths. Press lightly to mark the folds. Unfold the overskirt top. Use the chalk to mark the folds on the wrong side of the fabric.

Divide and mark the overskirt ruffle into eight equal parts.

Referring to **Diagram 9,** with right sides together, stitch the overskirt ruffle to the overskirt, following the directions on page 124 for gathering and attaching a ruffle. Press the seam allowances toward the overskirt.

Cut the shirring tape into eight 7″ (18cm) long pieces. Fold the ends of the pieces under 1″ (2.5cm). Use a straight pin to remove the cords from the

🧵 SEW SIMPLE

Use fusible shirring tape, such as Dritz iron-on 2-cord shirring tape, to speed up your sewing.

folded-under ends, as shown in **Diagram 10.** Trim the folded-under ends to ½″ (1.3cm).

Diagram 10

Center one piece of shirring tape over one marked line. Referring to **Diagram 11,** fold the ruffle seam allowance out of the way and match one end of the tape to the ruffle seam line; pin the tape in place. Stitch along both long edges of the tape, backstitching, as shown, at the ends of the tape. Tie the cords that are nearest to the center of the overskirt into a knot. Secure the knot with liquid fray preventer. Repeat for the other seven pieces of shirring tape.

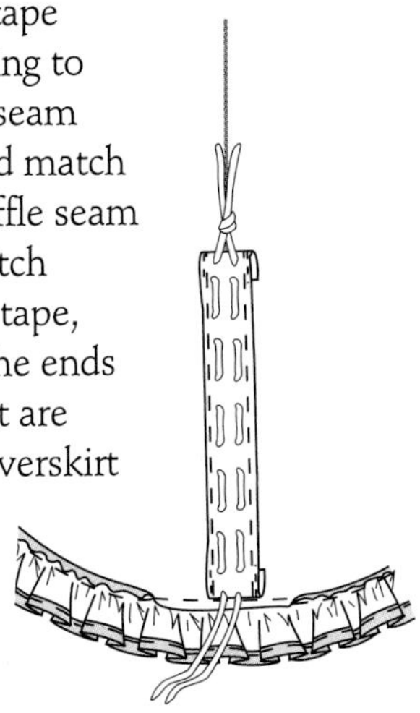

Diagram 11

INSTALLATION

Cover the table with the underskirt. Center the overskirt on the top of the table. Use books or other heavy objects to hold it in place. Pull on one set of shirring cords, gathering the overskirt to the desired depth. Tie the ends of the cords into a bow, and then tuck the bow up inside the overskirt. Repeat, gathering the remaining sets of cords to match, as shown in the photograph on page 14.

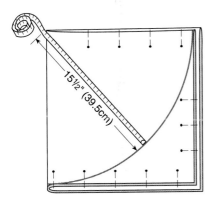

Diagram 7

Diagram 8

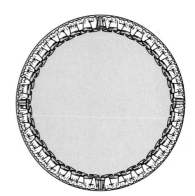

Diagram 9

There's more than one way to cover a round
table. A quick-sew covering and generous bow
are a winning combination.

ALL WRAPPED UP

Size:

To fit a 20″ (51cm) diameter × 25″ (63.5cm) high decorator table

To adjust these directions for a different size table, review the information on page 123 for customizing a tablecloth.

SUPPLIES

- *1 flat full-size print sheet**
- *1 flat full-size solid sheet**
- *1⅞ yards (1.8m) of 2″ (5cm) diameter piping cord*
- *One 20″ (51cm) square of ¼″ (6mm) thick foam core board*
- *Hot-glue gun and glue sticks*
- *Craft knife*
- *Tape measure*
- *Water-soluble marking pen*

*This project can also be made from 45″ (115cm) wide fabric. See "Design Plus" for additional information.

CUTTING DIRECTIONS

All measurements include ½″ (1.3cm) seam allowances.

From the print sheet, cut:

- *One 71″ (181cm) square tablecloth*
- *One 21″ (53.5cm) square table cover*

From the solid sheet, cut:

- *Two 6½″ × 70″ (16.5cm × 178cm) cord covers*
- *One 13″ × 24″ (33cm × 61cm) bow*
- *One 2¼″ × 4″ (5.7cm × 10cm) knot*
- *Two 11″ × 26″ (28cm × 66cm) tails*

⌖ DESIGN PLUS

To make this project from fabric instead of sheets, purchase 4½ yards (4.2m) of 45″ (115cm) wide print decorator fabric and 1⅝ yards (1.5m) of 45″ (115cm) wide solid decorator fabric.

From the print decorator fabric, cut:

- *Two 45″ × 71″ (115cm × 181cm) tablecloth panels*
- *One 21″ (53.5cm) square table cover*

Cut one 45″ × 71″ (115cm × 181cm) tablecloth panel lengthwise in half into two side panels. With right sides together, stitch one side panel to each side edge of the center panel, forming a 71″ × 88″ (181cm × 224cm) rectangle. Press the seams open. Follow the "Sewing Directions," beginning on page 20, substituting the rectangle for the 71″ (181cm) square in Step 1.

From the solid decorator fabric, cut:

- *Three 6½″ × 45″ (16.5cm × 115cm) cord covers*
- *One 13″ × 24″ (33cm × 61cm) bow*
- *One 2¼″ × 4″ (5.7cm × 10cm) knot*
- *Two 11″ × 26″ (28cm × 66cm) tails*

SEWING DIRECTIONS

1 Making the tablecloth

Fold the 71" (181cm) square in half and then in quarters, matching the cut edges. Pin the layers together at the cut edges. Using the tape measure and the marking pen, measure and mark a quarter-circle with a 35½" (90cm) radius, as shown in **Diagram 1.** Cut along the marked line, through all of the layers. Remove the pins and unfold the tablecloth.

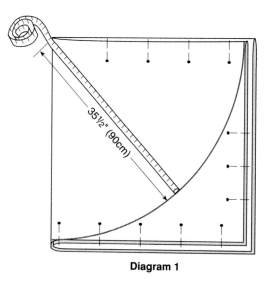

35½" (90cm)

Diagram 1

Referring to **Diagram 2,** press under ½" (1.3cm) on the edge of the tablecloth. Tuck the raw edge in to meet the crease. Press again. Stitch close to the second fold.

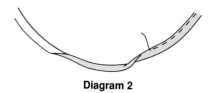

Diagram 2

🧵 SEW SIMPLE

Fuse the hem of the tablecloth, following the directions on page 127 for no-sew hemming.

2 Assembling the tabletop

Trace the top of the table onto the foam core. Use the craft knife to cut out the circle.

Fold the 21" (53.5cm) square table cover in half and then in quarters, matching the cut edges. Pin the layers together at the cut edges. Using the tape measure and the marking pen, measure and mark a quarter-circle with a 10½" (26.5cm) radius, as shown in **Diagram 3.** Cut along the marked line, through all of the layers. Remove the pins and unfold the cover.

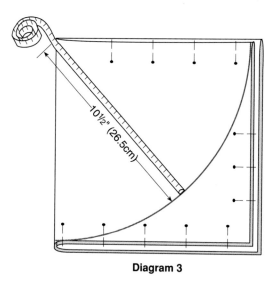

10½" (26.5cm)

Diagram 3

Center the cover, right side up, over the foam core top and glue it in place, as shown in **Diagram 4.**

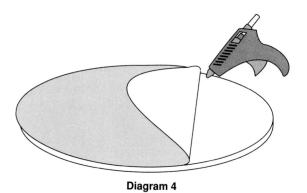

Diagram 4

3 Attaching the cord

Measure the circumference of the tabletop. Cut the cord to equal this measurement.

Stitch the cord cover sections together at the side edges to form one long cord cover. Press under 1″ (2.5cm) on one side edge.

Referring to **Diagram 5,** center the cord on the wrong side of the cord cover so that the end of the cord extends ½″ (1.3cm) beyond the unpressed side edge of the cover. Stitch the end of the cord to the cover.

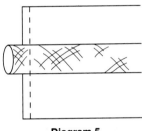

Diagram 5

Wrap the cover around the cord so that the long cut edges match. Using the machine zipper foot, stitch next to the cord for about 6″ (15cm). Raise the zipper foot, leaving the needle in the fabric. Use one hand to gently pull the cord. Use the other hand to slide the cover back toward the beginning of the stitching, as shown in **Diagram 6.** Repeat, stitching and then stopping to gather the cover every 6″ (15cm) until the cord is completely covered.

Referring to **Diagram 7,** join the ends of the cord by inserting the exposed end into the pressed-under edge of the cover. Slip stitch the cord cover ends together, following the directions on page 124 for slip stitching. Adjust the fullness so that the cover is evenly distributed.

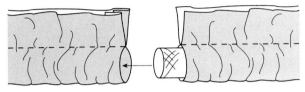

Diagram 7

Glue the cord in place around the rim of the covered tabletop, gluing the seam allowances to the underside of the foam core, as shown in **Diagram 8.**

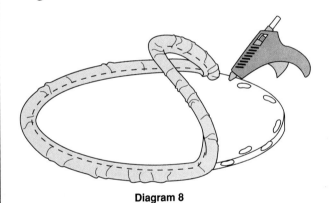

Diagram 8

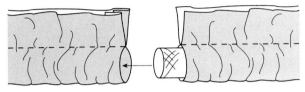

Diagram 6

4 Making the bow

Fold the bow piece in half lengthwise, with right sides together, and stitch the seam, as shown in **Diagram 9.** Turn the bow right side out and press.

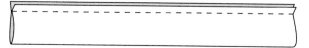

Diagram 9

Fold the bow in half crosswise and use the marking pen to mark at the fold. Unfold the bow. Overlap the ends slightly and then fold the bow in half crosswise, matching the center of the overlap to the mark.

Referring to **Diagram 10,** make two rows of hand-basting stitches at the center of the bow, through all of the layers. Pull up the threads, gathering the bow into two loops. Tie the thread ends to secure.

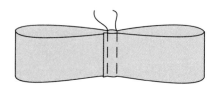

Diagram 10

Fold the knot piece in half lengthwise, with right sides together, and stitch the seam, as shown in **Diagram 11.** Turn the knot right side out and press.

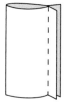

Diagram 11

Referring to **Diagram 12,** wrap the knot around the center of the bow and hand sew the edges together at the back of the bow.

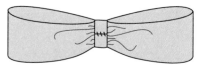

Diagram 12

Referring to **Diagram 13,** fold one tail piece in half lengthwise, with right sides together, and pin. Measure and mark along the cut edge 4" (10cm) from one side edge. Draw a line from this mark to the diagonally opposite corner. Cut along this line. Repeat for the other tail piece.

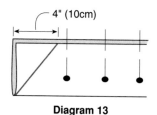

Diagram 13

Stitch ½" (1.3cm) from the long cut edge and the diagonal cut edge, through both layers, as shown in **Diagram 14.** Turn the tail right side out and press. Repeat for the other tail piece.

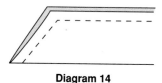

Diagram 14

Press a 1½" (3.8cm) long inverted pleat at the unstitched end, as shown in **Diagram 15.** Repeat for the other tail piece.

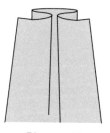

Diagram 15

Overlap and glue the pleated ends of the tails to the back of the bow.

INSTALLATION

Cover the table with the tablecloth, as shown in the photograph on page 18. Center the tabletop over the tablecloth. Glue the bow to the cord, covering the place where the cord ends are joined.

⊕ DESIGN PLUS

Decorator fabrics are usually treated with special soil-resistant finishes. To be sure, check the hang tags or read the information printed along the fabric's selvage edge. Untreated fabrics, including sheets and most apparel fabrics, can be protected with an at-home application of Scotchgard fabric protector, manufactured by The 3M Company. The 3M Company also operates a hot line offering assistance with any stain problem, even if the fabric was not treated with Scotchgard. Call 800-433-3296.

If your tastes run toward Victorian, you'll be inspired by this parlor-pretty covering reminiscent of eras past.

VICTORIAN SWAG

Size:

To fit a 20" (51cm) diameter × 25" (63.5cm) high decorator table

To adjust these directions for a different size table, review the information on page 123 for customizing a tablecloth.

SUPPLIES

- *4 yards (3.7m) of 45" to 60" (115cm to 153cm) wide decorator fabric, such as chintz, sateen, or polished cotton*
- *4 yards (3.7m) of 45" to 60" (115cm to 153cm) wide contrasting decorator fabric*
- *6¼ yards (5.8m) of 4" (10cm) wide fringe*
- *8¾ yards (8.1m) of 2-cord shirring tape*
- *Tape measure*
- *Water-soluble marking pen*
- *Dressmaker's chalk*
- *One 36" (91.5cm) long straight-edge ruler*
- *Liquid fray preventer*
- *12 small safety pins*

✥ DESIGN PLUS

For an ultra-feminine version of this tabletop duo, pair a moiré taffeta underskirt with a lace overskirt. Underline the lace with a lightweight fabric, color-matched to the taffeta, and substitute pregathered lace trim for the fringe.

CUTTING DIRECTIONS

All measurements include ½" (1.3cm) seam allowances.

From the decorator fabric, cut one 71" (181cm) long underskirt center panel from the full width of the fabric. Split the remaining fabric in half lengthwise and cut two 71" (181cm) long underskirt side panels.

From the contrasting decorator fabric, cut one 71" (181cm) long overskirt center panel from the full width of the fabric. Split the remaining fabric in half lengthwise and cut two 71" (181cm) long overskirt side panels.

SEWING DIRECTIONS

1 Assembling the underskirt

With right sides together, stitch one underskirt side panel to each side edge of the underskirt center panel, as shown in **Diagram 1.** Press the seams open.

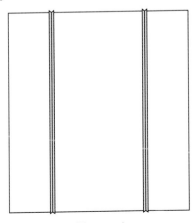

Diagram 1

Fold the underskirt in half and then in quarters, matching the cut edges. Pin the layers together at the cut edges. Using the tape measure and marking pen, measure and mark a quarter-circle with a 35½" (90cm) radius, as shown in **Diagram 2.** Cut along the marked line, through all of the layers.

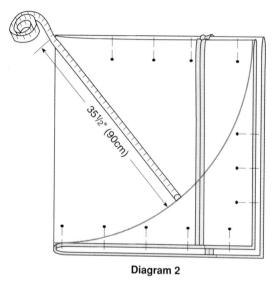

35½" (90cm)

Diagram 2

Remove the pins and unfold the underskirt.

Referring to **Diagram 3,** press under ½" (1.3cm) on the edge of the underskirt. Tuck the raw edge in to meet the crease. Press again. Stitch close to the second fold.

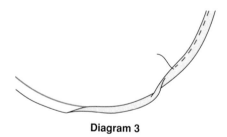

Diagram 3

2 Assembling the overskirt

With right sides together, stitch one overskirt side panel to each side edge of the overskirt center panel, as shown in **Diagram 1** on page 25. Press the seams open.

With wrong sides together, fold the overskirt in half and then in quarters, matching the cut edges. Pin the layers together at the cut edges. Using the tape measure and the marking pen, measure and mark a quarter-circle with a 35½" (90cm) radius, as shown in **Diagram 2.** Cut along the marked line, through all of the layers. Use the marking pen to mark the center of the overskirt. Remove the pins and unfold the overskirt.

Place the overskirt wrong side up on a large, flat surface. Referring to **Diagram 4,** make 12 marks, approximately 18" (45.5cm) apart, around the edge of the overskirt. Use the chalk and the straight-edge ruler to draw a line connecting each edge mark to the center mark.

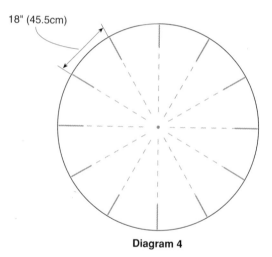

18" (45.5cm)

Diagram 4

🧵 SEW SIMPLE

To achieve a smooth, narrow hem on a curved edge, machine baste ½" (1.3cm) and ¼" (6mm) from the outer edge. Press under ½" (1.3cm) along the first row of stitches. Pull up the threads along the second row of stitches, easing the hem allowance to fit the curve of the fabric. Press the hem allowance flat. Tuck the raw edge in to meet the crease. Press again. Stitch close to the second fold.

Referring to **Diagram 3** on page 26, press under ½″ (1.3cm) on the edge of the overskirt. Tuck the raw edge in to meet the crease. Press again. Stitch close to the second fold.

3 Trimming the overskirt

Pin the fringe to the right side of the overskirt, matching the fringe header to the overskirt hem allowance and turning under the header ends and butting them together. Stitch along both long edges of the fringe header, through all of the layers, as shown in **Diagram 5.**

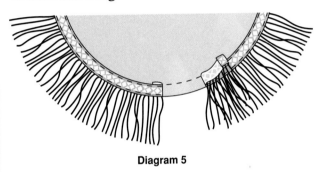

Diagram 5

Cut the shirring tape into twelve 26″ (66cm) long pieces. Fold the ends of the tapes under 1″ (2.5cm). Use a straight pin to remove the cords from the folded-under ends, as shown in **Diagram 6.** Trim the folded-under ends to ½″ (1.3cm).

Diagram 6

Referring to **Diagram 7,** center one piece of shirring tape over one marked line with the end of the tape 1″ (2.5cm) from the edge of the overskirt; pin the tape in place. Stitch along both long edges of the tape, backstitching at the ends of the tape, as shown. Tie the cords that are nearest to the center of the overskirt into a knot. Secure the knot with liquid fray preventer. Repeat for the other eleven pieces of shirring tape.

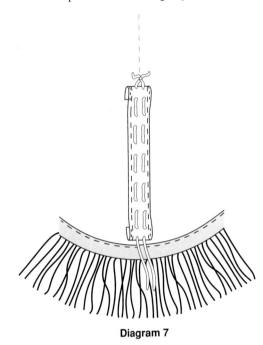

Diagram 7

INSTALLATION

Cover the table with the underskirt. Center the overskirt on the top of the table. Use books or other heavy objects to hold it in place. Pull on one set of shirring cords, gathering the overskirt to the desired depth. Tie the ends of the cords into a bow. Use a small safety pin to conceal the bow inside the overskirt. Repeat, gathering the remaining sets of cords to match, as shown in the photograph on page 24.

What can you do with a sheet and two pillowcases, besides make a bed? Create an attractive table topper!

FAST FUSED FLOWERS

Size:

To fit a 20″ (51cm) diameter × 25″ (63.5cm) high decorator table

To adjust these directions for a different size table, review the information on page 123 for customizing a tablecloth.

SUPPLIES

- *1 flat full-size sheet with a decorative border*
- *Two 20″ × 30″ (51cm × 76cm) standard-size pillowcases with decorative borders*
- *1½ yards (1.4m) of 18″ (45.5cm) wide paper-backed fusible web*
- *Seam ripper or small scissors*
- *Tape measure*
- *Water-soluble marking pen*

CUTTING DIRECTIONS

All measurements include ½″ (1.3cm) seam allowances.

Using the seam ripper or small scissors, rip out the hems on the pillowcases. Turn each pillowcase right side out and cut it open by cutting off the seam allowances close to the stitching. Cut off the hems at the lower edge of the sheet. Press the pillowcases and the sheet flat.

Draw a straight line across the sheet approximately 1″ (2.5cm) below the lower edge of the decorative border. Cut off the border strip along this line. Repeat for both pillowcases.

SEWING DIRECTIONS

1 Making the large tablecloth

Fold the sheet in half and then in quarters, matching the cut edges. Pin the layers together at the cut edges. Using the tape measure and marking pen, measure and mark a quarter-circle with a 35½″ (90cm) radius, as shown in **Diagram 1.** Cut along the marked line, through all of the layers. Remove the pins and unfold the tablecloth.

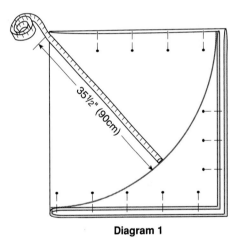

Diagram 1

Hem the edge of the tablecloth, following the directions on page 127 for no-sew hemming.

✦ DESIGN PLUS

Cut any remaining border strips into individual motifs. Fuse them at random intervals on the large or small tablecloth.

2 Assembling the small tablecloth

Cut one pillowcase in half crosswise into two side panels. With right sides together, fuse one side panel to each 40″ (102cm) edge of the other pillowcase, as shown in **Diagram 2** and following the directions on page 127 for no-sew seaming.

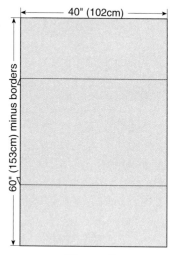

40″ (102cm)

60″ (153cm) minus borders

Diagram 2

Fold the pillowcases in half and then in quarters, matching the cut edges. Pin the layers together at the cut edges. Using the tape measure and marking pen, measure and mark a quarter-circle with a 17″ (43cm) radius, as shown in **Diagram 3**. Cut along the marked line, through all of the layers. Remove the pins and unfold the tablecloth.

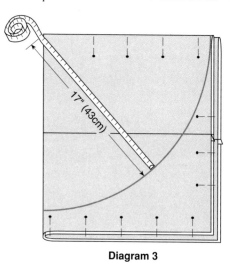

17″ (43cm)

Diagram 3

3 Applying the border

Apply the fusible web to the wrong side of each border strip, following the fusible web manufacturer's directions. Cut out the border, following the edges of the motifs. Peel off the paper backing. Referring to **Diagram 4,** position the border on the small tablecloth, matching the outer edge of the border to the outer edge of the tablecloth. Cut the motifs apart, as necessary, so that the border follows the curve of the tablecloth. Fuse the border in place, following the fusible web manufacturer's directions. Trim the edge of the tablecloth to match the edge of the border.

Diagram 4

INSTALLATION

Cover the table with the large tablecloth. Cover the top of the table with the small tablecloth, as shown in the photograph on page 28.

COVER ME PRETTY

*Star appliqués in Christmas print fabrics
bring cheer to your holiday table.*

NORTH STAR APPLIQUÉ

Size:

To fit a 28" to 48" × 46" to 104" (71cm to 122cm × 117cm to 264cm) rectangular dining table

SUPPLIES

- *45" (115cm) or 60" (153cm) wide cotton or cotton/polyester solid or print fabric for the tablecloth**
- *Four 45" (115cm) or 60" (153cm) wide cotton or cotton/polyester holiday print fabrics for the appliqués**
- *45" (115cm) or 60" (153cm) wide cotton or cotton/polyester print fabric for the binding**
- *18" (45.5cm) wide paper-backed fusible web**
- *Gold metallic machine embroidery thread*
- *Tracing paper (optional)*
- *Lightweight cardboard*
- *Craft knife or single-edge razor blade*
- *Pencil*
- *Water-soluble marking pen*
- *One 36" (91.5cm) straight-edge ruler*

*See the "Cutting Directions" for additional information.

CUTTING DIRECTIONS

All measurements include ½" (1.3cm) seam allowances.

This tablecloth is designed to have at least a 14" (35.5cm) drop on all four sides of the table. Measure the width and length of your table. Consult the Yardage Chart on page 37 to locate the size tablecloth that is at least 28" (71cm) wider and 28" (71cm) longer than your table. Purchase the amount of tablecloth fabric, appliqué fabric, binding fabric, and paper-backed fusible web listed for your size tablecloth.

Before cutting, review the information on page 123 for preshrinking fabric and trim.

From the 45" or 60" (115cm or 153cm) wide tablecloth fabric, cut one center panel and two side panels, as indicated in the Cutting Chart on page 37 for your size tablecloth.

From the binding fabric, cut 2½" (6.3cm) wide × 45" or 60" (115cm or 153cm) long strips, as indicated in the Cutting Chart on page 37 for your size tablecloth.

SEWING DIRECTIONS

1 Assembling the tablecloth

With right sides together, stitch one side panel to each side edge of the center panel, as shown in **Diagram 1.** Press the seams open. Note: For a 60" × 84" (153cm × 214cm) tablecloth from 60" (153cm) wide fabric, there are no side panels.

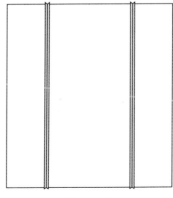

Diagram 1

2 Creating the appliqués

Using the tracing paper or a photocopy machine, copy the full-size appliqué pattern shown in **Diagram 2.** Cut out the pattern and trace it onto the cardboard. Use the craft knife or razor blade to cut out the cardboard template.

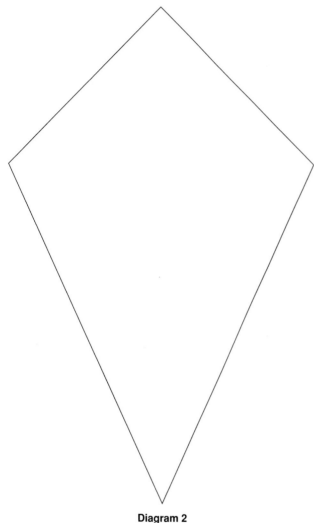

Diagram 2

Note: Pattern shown is actual size.

✦ DESIGN PLUS

For a year-round tablecloth, choose coordinating fabrics in prints that match your decor or complement your table settings.

Using the pencil and the template, trace the number of appliqué shapes listed in the Cutting Chart on page 37 for your size tablecloth onto the paper side of the paper-backed fusible web. Cut out the appliqué shapes, leaving a small margin of paper-backed fusible web all around the traced outlines. Do not remove the paper backing. Apply the appliqué shapes to the wrong side of one appliqué fabric, following the fusible web manufacturer's directions. Cut out each shape on the traced outline. Repeat for the other three appliqué fabrics. Remove the paper backing from each shape.

Referring to **Diagram 3** and working on the right side of the tablecloth, use the ruler and marking pen to measure and mark a line that is 7″ (18cm) from one edge. Repeat for the other three sides. Locate and mark the center of each line.

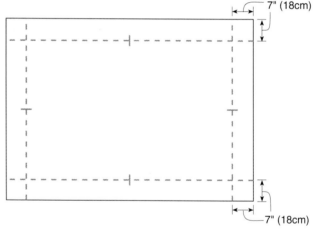

7″ (18cm)

7″ (18cm)

Diagram 3

Divide the length measurement of one long edge of the tablecloth by 12. Repeat for the width measurement. When the answer is an even number, there will be an even number of stars along that edge. When the answer is an odd number, there will be an odd number of stars along that edge.

Pin the appliqué shapes along the marked line, forming a row of stars with the points touching.

🧵 SEW SIMPLE

To ensure an extra-strong bond, fuse the appliqué shapes in place as directed. Then turn the tablecloth over and repeat the fusing process, applying the recommended amount of heat, steam, and moisture to the wrong side of the fabric.

For even greater durability, stitch around the appliqué shapes using machine embroidery thread and a short, wide machine zigzag stitch. Use tear-away stabilizer underneath the appliqués. When the stitching is finished, gently tear away the stabilizer.

Use four shapes for each star, alternating the fabrics, as shown in **Diagrams 4** and **5.** For an even number of stars, position two stars so that the tips meet at the center mark, as shown in **Diagram 4.** For an odd number of stars, match the center of the first star to the center mark, as shown in **Diagram 5.** Repeat, arranging stars along the other three edges so that the tips meet all around the tablecloth. Fuse the stars in place, following the fusible web manufacturer's directions.

Set your sewing machine for a medium-length, medium-width zigzag stitch. Use the metallic thread in the top of the machine; match the bobbin thread to the tablecloth fabric. Stitch all around each appliqué shape, as shown in **Diagram 6.**

Diagram 6

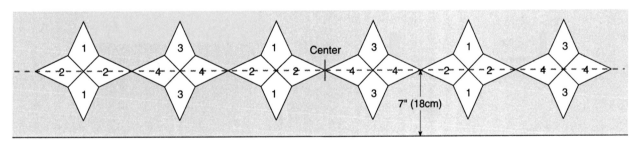

Diagram 4

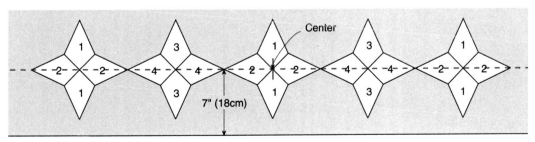

Diagram 5

3 Applying the binding

With right sides together, stitch the binding strips together at the ends to form one long strip. Press the seams open. Cut the strip into four sections—two equal to the tablecloth width plus 1" (2.5cm) and two equal to the tablecloth length plus 1" (2.5cm).

Press the ends of one strip under ½" (1.3cm) and stitch ⅜" (1cm) from the folds. Fold the strip in half lengthwise and press. Open the strip and fold one long edge under ¼" (6mm) and press, as shown in **Diagram 7**. Repeat for the other three strips.

With the right side of the binding to the wrong side of the tablecloth and with raw edges even, pin one long strip to one long edge of the tablecloth. Stitch ¼" (6mm) from the raw edges, as shown in **Diagram 8,** and then press the binding toward the seam allowances. Refold the binding along the lengthwise fold and pin in place. On the right side of the tablecloth, topstitch along the inner edge of the binding, through all of the layers, as shown in **Diagram 9**. Repeat for the opposite long edge. Repeat for the two short edges, overlapping the ends at the corners, as shown in **Diagram 10**.

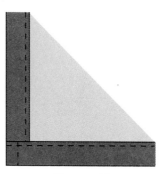

Diagram 10

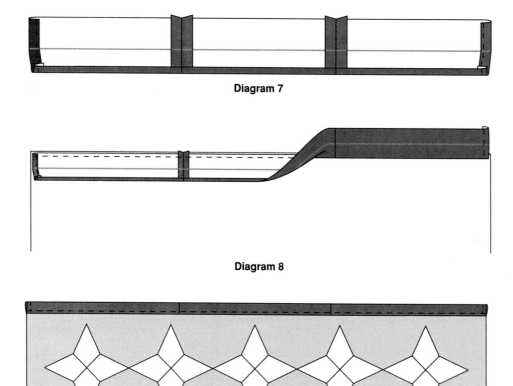

Diagram 7

Diagram 8

Diagram 9

YARDAGE CHART

TABLECLOTH SIZE	45″ (115CM) WIDE FABRIC			60″ (153CM) WIDE FABRIC			FUSIBLE WEB
	TABLECLOTH	APPLIQUÉS*	BINDING**	TABLECLOTH	APPLIQUÉS*	BINDING**	
A: 60″ × 84″ (153cm × 214cm)	4¾ yards (4.4m)	½ yard (0.5m)	⅝ yard (0.6m)	2⅜ yards (2.2m)	½ yard (0.5m)	½ yard (0.5m)	3½ yards (3.3m)
B: 72″ × 84″ (183cm × 214cm)	4¾ yards (4.4m)	½ yard (0.5m)	⅝ yard (0.6m)	4¾ yards (4.4m)	½ yard (0.5m)	½ yard (0.5m)	4 yards (3.7m)
C: 72″ × 96″ (183cm × 244cm)	5⅜ yards (5m)	½ yard (0.5m)	¾ yard (0.7m)	5⅜ yards (5m)	½ yard (0.5m)	½ yard (0.5m)	4 yards (3.7m)
D: 72″ × 108″ (183cm × 275cm)	6 yards (5.5m)	½ yard (0.5m)	¾ yard (0.7m)	6 yards (5.5m)	½ yard (0.5m)	½ yard (0.5m)	4½ yards (4.2m)
E: 84″ × 108″ (214cm × 275cm)	6 yards (5.5m)	½ yard (0.5m)	¾ yard (0.7m)	6 yards (5.5m)	½ yard (0.5m)	⅝ yard (0.6m)	5 yards (4.6m)
F: 72″ × 120″ (183cm × 305cm)	6¾ yards (6.2m)	½ yard (0.5m)	¾ yard (0.7m)	6¾ yards (6.2m)	½ yard (0.5m)	⅝ yard (0.6m)	5 yards (4.6m)
G: 84″ × 120″ (214cm × 305cm)	6¾ yards (6.2m)	½ yard (0.5m)	⅞ yard (0.8m)	6¾ yards (6.2m)	½ yard (0.5m)	⅝ yard (0.6m)	5 yards (4.6m)
H: 84″ × 132″ (214cm × 335cm)	7⅜ yards (6.8m)	½ yard (0.5m)	⅞ yard (0.8m)	7⅜ yards (6.8m)	½ yard (0.5m)	¾ yard (0.7m)	5½ yards (5.1m)

* Amount given is for each of four different print fabrics.

**Choose a binding fabric to match one of the appliqué fabrics.

CUTTING CHART

TABLECLOTH SIZE*	45″ (115CM) WIDE FABRIC			60″ (153CM) WIDE FABRIC			APPLIQUÉ SHAPES**
	CENTER PANEL	SIDE PANELS	BINDING STRIPS	CENTER PANEL	SIDE PANELS	BINDING STRIPS	
A	32″ × 84″ (81.5cm × 214cm)	14½″ × 84″ (37cm × 214cm)	7	60″ × 84″ (153cm × 214cm)	—	5	20
B	45″ × 84″ (115cm × 214cm)	14½″ × 84″ (37cm × 214cm)	8	45″ × 84″ (115cm × 214cm)	14½″ × 84″ (37cm × 214cm)	6	22
C	45″ × 96″ (115cm × 244cm)	14½″ × 96″ (37cm × 244cm)	8	45″ × 96″ (115cm × 244cm)	14½″ × 96″ (37cm × 244cm)	6	24
D	45″ × 108″ (115cm × 275cm)	14½″ × 108″ (37cm × 275cm)	9	45″ × 108″ (115cm × 275cm)	14½″ × 108″ (37cm × 275cm)	7	26
E	45″ × 108″ (115cm × 275cm)	20½″ × 108″ (52cm × 275cm)	9	57″ × 108″ (145cm × 275cm)	14½″ × 108″ (37cm × 275cm)	7	28
F	45″ × 120″ (115cm × 305cm)	14½″ × 120″ (37cm × 305cm)	9	45″ × 120″ (115cm × 305cm)	14½″ × 120″ (37cm × 305cm)	7	28
G	45″ × 120″ (115cm × 305cm)	20½″ × 120″ (52cm × 305cm)	10	57″ × 120″ (145cm × 305cm)	14½″ × 120″ (37cm × 305cm)	7	30
H	45″ × 132″ (115cm × 335cm)	20½″ × 132″ (52cm × 335cm)	10	57″ × 132″ (145cm × 335cm)	14½″ × 132″ (37cm × 335cm)	8	32

* See the Yardage Chart above for the tablecloth dimensions that correspond to these letter codes.

**Number given is for each of four different print fabrics.

Liven up even the simplest of table coverings with quick-and-easy stencils in the colors of spring.

PAINTED POSIES

Size:

To fit a 28" to 48" × 46" to 104" (71cm to 122cm × 117cm to 264cm) rectangular table

SUPPLIES

- *45" (115cm) or 60" (153cm) wide cotton or cotton/polyester fabric**
- *Extra-wide double-fold bias tape**
- *Tape measure*
- *Water-soluble marking pen*

STENCILING

- *Oiled stencil paper or stencil acetate*
- *Graphite paper for transferring the design*
- *Craft knife*
- *Two to six ½" (1.3cm) flat stencil brushes*
- *Fine-tip paintbrush*
- *7 colors of stencil paint cream, such as Stencil Magic (here, we used green, pink, purple, red, yellow, orange, and blue)*
- *Green permanent-ink fabric pen*
- *Soap and water or turpentine to clean the brushes, as directed by the paint manufacturer*
- *Fixative spray, such as Krylon*

*See the "Cutting Directions" for additional information.

CUTTING DIRECTIONS

All measurements include ½" (1.3cm) seam allowances.

This tablecloth is designed to have at least a 12" (30.5cm) drop on all four sides of the table. Measure the width and length of your table. Consult the Yardage Chart on page 40 to locate the size tablecloth that is at least 24" (61cm) wider and 24" (61cm) longer than your table. Purchase the amount of 45" (115cm) or 60" (153cm) wide fabric and extra-wide double-fold bias tape listed for your size tablecloth.

Before cutting, review the information on page 123 for preshrinking fabric and trim.

From the 45" or 60" (115cm or 153cm) wide fabric, cut one center panel and two side panels, as indicated in the Cutting Chart on page 40 for your size tablecloth.

SEWING DIRECTIONS

1 Assembling the tablecloth

With right sides together, stitch one side panel to each side edge of the center panel, as shown in **Diagram 1**. Press the seams open. Note: For a 60" (153cm) square tablecloth or a 60" × 84" (153cm × 214cm) rectangular tablecloth from 60" (153cm) wide fabric, there are no side panels.

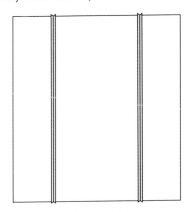

Diagram 1

YARDAGE CHART

TABLECLOTH SIZE	45" (115CM) WIDE FABRIC	60" (153CM) WIDE FABRIC	BIAS TAPE
A: 60" (153cm) square	3⅜ yards (3.1m)	1¾ yards (1.7m)	7 yards (6.5m)
B: 60" × 84" (153cm × 214cm)	4¾ yards (4.4m)	2⅜ yards (2.2m)	8⅛ yards (7.5m)
C: 72" × 84" (183cm × 214cm)	4¾ yards (4.4m)	4¾ yards (4.4m)	8¾ yards (8.1m)
D: 72" × 96" (183cm × 244cm)	5⅜ yards (5m)	5⅜ yards (5m)	9½ yards (8.8m)
E: 72" × 108" (183cm × 275cm)	6 yards (5.5m)	6 yards (5.5m)	10⅛ yards (9.4m)
F: 84" × 108" (214cm × 275cm)	6 yards (5.5m)	6 yards (5.5m)	10¾ yards (10m)
G: 72" × 120" (183cm × 305cm)	6¾ yards (6.2m)	6¾ yards (6.2m)	10¾ yards (10m)
H: 84" × 120" (214cm × 305cm)	6¾ yards (6.2m)	6¾ yards (6.2m)	11⅞ yards (10.6m)
I: 84" × 132" (214cm × 335cm)	7⅜ yards (6.8m)	7⅜ yards (6.8m)	12½ yards (11.7m)

CUTTING CHART

TABLECLOTH SIZE*	45" (115CM) WIDE FABRIC		60" (153CM) WIDE FABRIC	
	CENTER PANEL	SIDE PANELS	CENTER PANEL	SIDE PANELS
A	32" × 60" (81.5cm × 153cm)	14½" × 60" (37cm × 153cm)	60" × 60" (153cm × 153cm)	—
B	32" × 84" (81.5cm × 214cm)	14½" × 84" (37cm × 214cm)	60" × 84" (153cm × 214cm)	—
C	45" × 84" (115cm × 214cm)	14½" × 84" (37cm × 214cm)	45" × 84" (115cm × 214cm)	14½" × 84" (37cm × 214cm)
D	45" × 96" (115cm × 244cm)	14½" × 96" (37cm × 244cm)	45" × 96" (115cm × 244cm)	14½" × 96" (37cm × 244cm)
E	45" × 108" (115cm × 275cm)	14½" × 108" (37cm × 275cm)	45" × 108" (115cm × 275cm)	14½" × 108" (37cm × 275cm)
F	45" × 108" (115cm × 275cm)	20½" × 108" (52cm × 275cm)	57" × 108" (145cm × 275cm)	14½" × 108" (37cm × 275cm)
G	45" × 120" (115cm × 305cm)	14½" × 120" (37cm × 305cm)	45" × 120" (115cm × 305cm)	14½" × 120" (37cm × 305cm)
H	45" × 120" (115cm × 305cm)	20½" × 120" (52cm × 305cm)	57" × 120" (145cm × 305cm)	14½" × 120" (37cm × 305cm)
I	45" × 132" (115cm × 335cm)	20½" × 132" (52cm × 335cm)	57" × 132" (145cm × 335cm)	14½" × 132" (37cm × 335cm)

*See the Yardage Chart above for the tablecloth dimensions that correspond to these letter codes.

With the wrong sides together, fold the tablecloth in half and then in quarters, matching the cut edges. Lightly press the tablecloth to mark the folds. Use the marking pen to mark the center of the tablecloth. Unfold the tablecloth and place it on a large, flat surface. Referring to **Diagram 2,** use the tape measure and marking pen to mark a circle with an 8″ (20.5cm) radius. Use the marking pen to mark along each fold at the circle and for about 2″ (5cm) from the cut edges of the tablecloth.

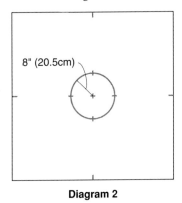

Diagram 2

2 Applying the binding

With right sides together, stitch the ends of the double-fold bias tape together to form one long strip, following the directions on page 124 for joining bias strips.

Referring to the photograph on page 38, apply the bias tape to the edges of the tablecloth, following the directions on page 125 for applying double-fold bias tape.

🧵 SEW SIMPLE

For faster stenciling, purchase one stencil brush for each paint color. This eliminates time spent washing and drying brushes between colors. It also ensures that you start each color with a dry brush. Using a damp brush can cause the paint to run under the stencil.

Spread the tablecloth out on a large, flat surface so that you can stencil the entire border without moving the tablecloth. This way, all of the paints can dry at the same time.

STENCILING DIRECTIONS

1 Preparing the stencils

Before you begin, review the information on page 127 in "Stenciling." Using **Diagrams 3** and **4** on this page and **Diagrams 5, 6,** and **7** on page 42, prepare the stencils for the tulips and the hyacinths as directed.

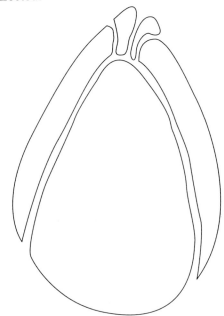

Note: Patterns shown are actual size.   **Diagram 3**

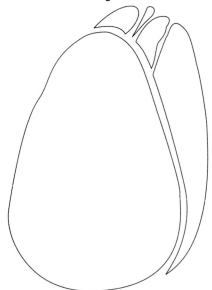

Diagram 4

Diagram 5

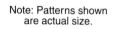

Note: Patterns shown
are actual size.

Diagram 6

Diagram 7

2 Applying the design

Stencil a ring of tulips around the marked circle at the center of the tablecloth, using the open and closed tulips and varying the paint colors as desired. Begin by stenciling one tulip at each quarter mark, positioning each tulip so that the bottom of the flower just rests on the circle, as shown in **Diagram 8**. Stencil three tulips in each of the spaces along the circle between the first tulips.

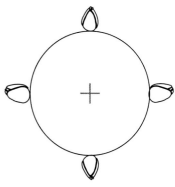

Diagram 8

Referring to **Diagrams 9** and **10** and the photograph on page 38, stencil one large closed tulip approximately 12″ (30.5cm) from one corner. Stencil two small closed tulips, placing one on each side and approximately 2″ (5cm) below the first tulip.

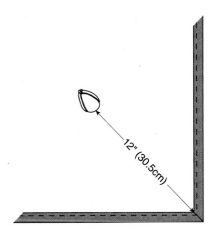

Diagram 9

Using the marking pen and referring to **Diagram 10**, sketch in the stems and leaves. When you are satisfied with the results, use the green permanent-ink fabric pen to draw the stems and outline the leaves. Using the fine-tip brush and green paint, fill

in the leaf design. Repeat for the opposite corner of the tablecloth. Repeat for the two remaining corners of the tablecloth, using the open tulips.

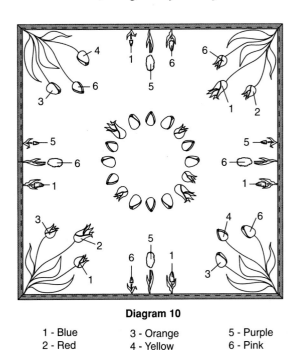

Diagram 10

| 1 - Blue | 3 - Orange | 5 - Purple |
| 2 - Red | 4 - Yellow | 6 - Pink |

Referring to **Diagram 10** and the photograph on page 38, position the hyacinth stencil at one edge of the cloth, matching the center hyacinth to the center mark and placing the ends of the stems just above the binding. Stencil the stems, using the green paint. Using the pink, purple, and blue paints, stencil the flowers, making each a different color.

Let the paints dry thoroughly. Remove the ink from the tablecloth, following the marking pen manufacturer's directions.

Apply the fixative spray to the finished design, following the fixative spray manufacturer's directions.

✴ DESIGN PLUS

If the edge of the tablecloth is 84″ (214cm) or wider, stencil three sets of hyacinths along the edge. Place one set at the center mark and one set midway between the center mark and each corner.

Bold, bright stripes add just the right touch to a table set for a birthday celebration.

YIPES! STRIPES!

Size:

To fit a 28″ to 48″ (71cm to 122cm) × 46″ to 104″ (117cm to 264cm) rectangular table

SUPPLIES

- *45″ (115cm) wide cotton or cotton/polyester fabric with vertical stripes**

*See the "Cutting Directions" for additional information.

CUTTING DIRECTIONS

All measurements include ½″ (1.3cm) seam allowances.

This tablecloth is designed to have a 13½″ (34.5cm) drop on all four sides. Measure the width and length of your table. Consult the Yardage/Cutting Chart to locate the size table that comes closest to, but does not exceed, your table's width and length measurements. Purchase the amount of fabric listed for that size table.

Before cutting, review the information on page 123 for preshrinking fabric and trim.

From the fabric, cut:

- *1 rectangle that is 1″ (2.5cm) wider and 1″ (2.5cm) longer than your table measurement. Note: If your table is more than 44″ (112cm) wide, see "Design Plus" on page 46.*

- *14½″ (37cm) long ruffle sections. Cut the number of ruffle sections indicated in the Yardage/Cutting Chart for your approximate table size. Use the full width of the fabric for each ruffle section.*

YARDAGE/CUTTING CHART		
APPROXIMATE TABLE SIZE	**45″ (115CM) WIDE FABRIC**	**RUFFLE SECTIONS**
28″ × 46″ (71cm × 117cm)	5 yards (4.6m)	9
40″ × 54″ (102cm × 136cm)	6 yards (5.5m)	11
36″ × 60″ (91.5cm × 153cm)	6¼ yards (5.8m)	11
48″ × 72″ (122cm × 183cm)	10 yards (9.2m)	14
36″ × 74″ (91.5cm × 188cm)	7½ yards (6.9m)	13
48″ × 90″ (122cm × 229cm)	11½ yards (10.7m)	16
36″ × 94″ (91.5cm × 239cm)	8¾ yards (8.1m)	15
48″ × 104″ (122cm × 264cm)	12¾ yards (11.8m)	17

🧵 SEW SIMPLE

To eliminate the possibility of the machine-basting threads breaking during gathering, do not machine baste along the raw edge of the ruffle. Instead, set your sewing machine for a wide zigzag stitch. Cut a piece of strong, thin cord, such as pearl cotton or lightweight packing string, which is slightly longer than the raw edge of the ruffle. Position the cord within the seam allowance and zigzag over it so that the left swing of the needle falls just within the seam allowance and the cord is not caught in the stitches. When you are ready to attach the ruffle, gather the ruffle by pulling up the cord.

SEWING DIRECTIONS

1 Preparing the top

Divide and mark the edge of the top into 16 equal parts.

2 Assembling the ruffle

Referring to **Diagram 1,** with right sides together, stitch the ruffle sections together at the ends to form one continuous ruffle. Press the seams open.

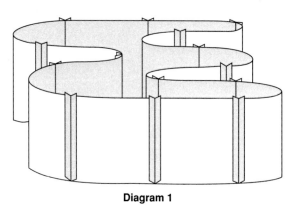

Diagram 1

Referring to **Diagram 2,** press under ½″ (1.3cm) on one long edge. Tuck the raw edge in to meet the crease. Press again. Stitch close to the second fold.

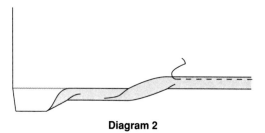

Diagram 2

Machine baste along the raw edge, following the directions on page 124 for preparing a ruffle. Divide and mark the ruffle into 16 equal parts.

⊕ DESIGN PLUS

For tables that are more than 44″ (112cm) wide, cut two panels of fabric, each equal to the length of the table plus 1″ (2.5cm). Use the full width of the fabric for each panel. Split one panel in half lengthwise for two side panels.

With right sides together, stitch one side panel to each side edge of the center panel, as shown in Diagram 1 on page 25. If necessary, adjust the width of the panels before stitching so that the color bars continue in an unbroken sequence across the width of the joined panels. Press the seams open. Cut an equal amount off each side edge so that the width of the joined panels equals the width of the tabletop plus 1″ (2.5cm). Use the leftover fabric to make the napkins on page 62 or the basket cover on page 116.

3 Attaching the ruffle

Referring to **Diagram 3,** with right sides together, stitch the ruffle to the top, following the directions on page 124 for gathering and attaching a ruffle.

Press the ruffle and ruffle seam allowances down, away from the top of the tablecloth.

⊕ DESIGN PLUS

For a more formal tablecloth, extend the length of the ruffle to the floor. Measure the height of the table from the edge of the tabletop to the floor and then subtract 13½" (34.5cm). Multiply this additional length by the number of ruffle panels listed in the Yardage/Cutting Chart on page 45 for your approximate table size. Now divide by 360 (91.5cm). This will tell you how many more yards (meters) of fabric to purchase.

Cut each ruffle section equal to the height of the table plus ½" (1.3cm). Use the full width of the fabric for each ruffle section.

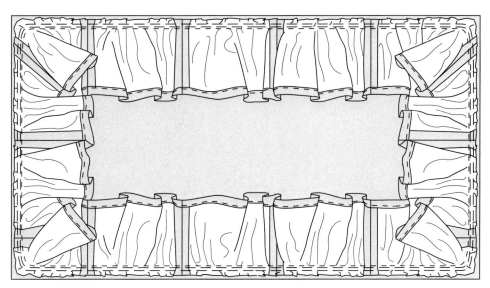

Diagram 3

Let your artistic talents shine when
you create a one-of-a-kind tablecloth
with the flick of a paintbrush.

A PATCH OF COLOR

Size:

To fit a 36″ (91.5cm) diameter round table or a 28″ to 40″ (71cm to 102cm) square table

SUPPLIES

- 1⅞ yards (1.8m) of 60″ (153cm) wide cotton or linen white fabric
- 7 yards (6.5m) of extra-wide double-fold bias tape
- 5 colors of fabric paint (here, we used blue, green, purple, pink, and yellow)
- Natural bristle paintbrush
- Dressmaker's chalk
- One 36″ (91.5cm) straight-edge ruler

⊕ DESIGN PLUS

To make this tablecloth from 45″ (115cm) wide fabric, purchase 3⅜ yards (3.1m) of fabric. Cut:

- *One 32″ × 60″ (81.5cm × 153cm) center panel*
- *Two 14½″ × 60″ (37cm × 153cm) side panels*

With right sides together and using ½″ (1.3cm) seam allowances, stitch one side panel to each 60″ (153cm) edge of the center panel, as shown in Diagram 1 on page 25. Press the seams open.

CUTTING DIRECTIONS

Before cutting, review the information on page 123 for preshrinking fabric and trim.

From the white fabric, cut one 60″ (153cm) square tablecloth.

PAINTING DIRECTIONS

Spread out the tablecloth on a large, flat surface. Use the ruler and the chalk to measure and mark a grid of 4″ (10cm) squares. Referring to **Diagram 1** as a guide, fill in some of the squares with fabric paint, using each paint color in approximately 12 squares. Use light, feathery, parallel brush strokes to apply the paint in one direction.

		1	2	3			3			2			4	
4				5				1				1		
					1	4					3		2	
2			3				5		5			4		
				5			2			1			1	
	1									3				
5		2				3			4			5		
			4											
3					1		5				1			4
5		4					2					4		
		2		2										
3					5			1			2			
	1						3						1	3
4				2	4			5		3				
5			4						3			2		5

Diagram 1

1 - Blue   4 - Pink
2 - Green   5 - Yellow
3 - Purple

Repeat, working at right angles to the first set of strokes, as shown in **Diagram 2.** Work one paint color at a time. Wash and dry the brush between colors.

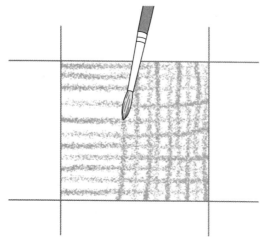

Diagram 2

Let the paint dry. Heat set the paint colors, following the paint manufacturer's directions.

SEWING DIRECTIONS

Apply bias tape to the edges of the tablecloth, following the directions on page 125 for applying double-fold bias tape.

Wash the finished tablecloth to remove the chalk markings.

🧵 SEW SIMPLE

Practice your brush stroke technique on scraps of the fabric before applying paint to the tablecloth.

PLACE SETTINGS

*E*asy, pleat-it-yourself trim transforms simple oval place mats into stylish accessories.

PLEATED TO PLEASE

Size:

Four 11″ × 17″ (28cm × 43cm) oval place mats, excluding the trim

SUPPLIES

- *1½ yards (1.4m) of 45″ (115cm) wide print fabric, such as broadcloth, linen, calico, or chintz*
- *1¾ yards (1.7m) of 45″ (115cm) wide solid fabric*
- *¾ yard (0.7m) of 45″ (115cm) wide polyester batting*
- *Fabric pleater, such as Perfect Pleater**
- *Water-soluble marking pen*
- *Straight-edge ruler*
- *One 20″ × 26″ (51cm × 66cm) sheet of tissue paper*
- *Pencil*
- *Fabric glue, such as Aleene's OK to Wash It*

*If you can't find Perfect Pleater at local fabric or craft stores, you can order it through Nancy's Notions, Ltd., P.O. Box 683, Beaver Dam, WI 53916-9976; 800-833-0690.

CUTTING DIRECTIONS

Before cutting, review the information on page 123 for preshrinking fabric and trim.

Fold the tissue paper in half and then in quarters, matching the cut edges. Crease the folds. Unfold the tissue paper. Using the tissue paper and **Diagram 1** on page 54, match the tissue paper folds to the fold lines on the diagram. Using the

pencil, trace the place mat cutting line onto the tissue paper, as shown in **Diagram 2**. Refold the tissue paper and cut along the marked line, through all of the layers of paper. Unfold the paper pattern.

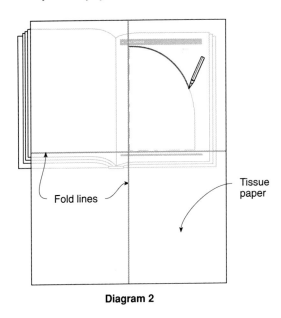

Fold lines

Tissue paper

Diagram 2

From the print fabric, cut:

- *Four 13″ × 19″ (33cm × 48.5cm) place mat fronts*
- *Four 13″ × 19″ (33cm × 48.5cm) place mat backs*

From the solid fabric, cut:

- *Eight 4″ × 45″ (10cm × 115cm) trim sections*
- *Four 4″ × 30″ (10cm × 76cm) trim sections*
- *11 yards (10.2m) of 2″ (5cm) wide bias strips, following the directions on page 125 for making continuous bias strips. Cut the bias strip into eight 50″ (127cm) lengths.*

From the batting, cut four 13″ × 19″ (33cm × 48.5cm) batting sections.

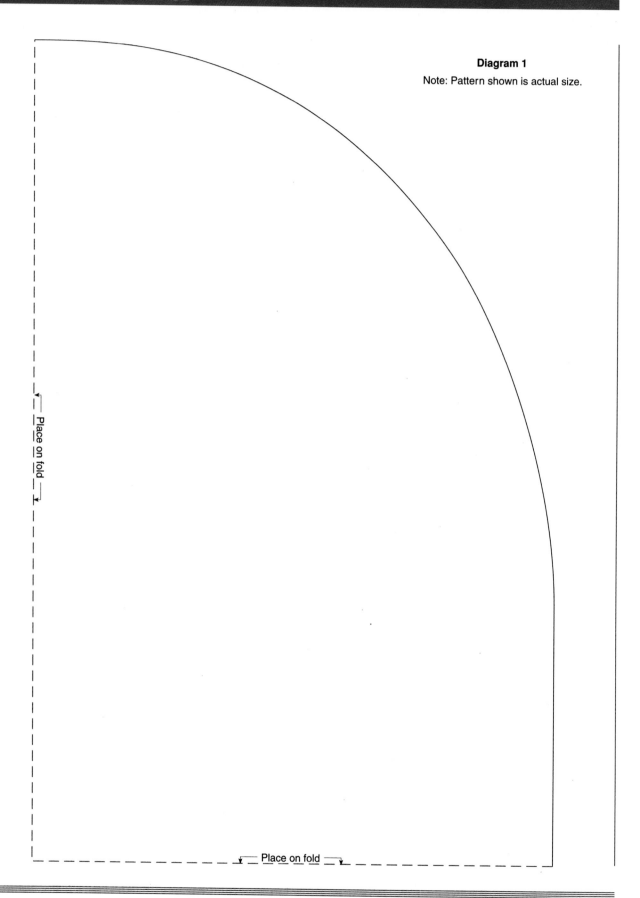

Diagram 1

Note: Pattern shown is actual size.

Place on fold

Place on fold

SEWING DIRECTIONS

Follow these directions for each place mat.

1 Marking the quilting lines

With right sides together, fold down one corner of one place mat front until the adjacent lengthwise and crosswise edges meet, as shown in **Diagram 3.** Press along the fold. Unfold the place mat front. Using the marking pen, mark the fold.

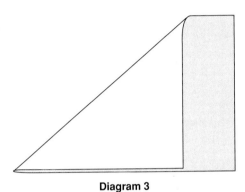

Diagram 3

Using the ruler and the marking pen, draw a parallel line 2½″ (6.3cm) from the first line. Repeat, covering the place mat front with parallel lines that are 2½″ (6.3cm) apart. Repeat, folding down an adjacent corner, as shown in **Diagram 4,** and then drawing parallel lines that intersect with the first set of diagonal lines.

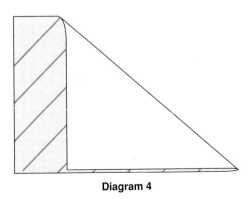

Diagram 4

2 Quilting the place mat

Working on a large, flat surface, place one place mat back wrong side up. Place one batting section on top of the place mat back. Place one place mat front, right side up, over the batting. Pin the layers together at frequent intervals. Set the sewing machine stitch length for eight to ten stitches per inch (2.5cm). Machine stitch along the marked lines, through all of the layers, as shown in **Diagram 5.**

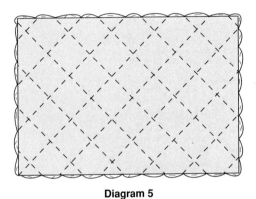

Diagram 5

Center the paper pattern over the quilted place mat. Trim the edges of the place mat to match the paper pattern.

🧵 SEW SIMPLE

Purchase prequilted fabric or have your chosen fabric quilted commercially. If your local fabric store doesn't offer this service, ask someone there to refer you to a store that does.

3 Pleating the trim

Referring to **Diagram 6,** with right sides together, stitch one 30″ (76cm) long and two 45″ (115cm) long trim sections together at the ends to form one long strip. Press the seams open. Press under ½″ (1.3cm) on one end. With wrong sides together, fold the strip in half lengthwise. Press. Baste the layers together ⅜″ (1cm) from the long raw edges.

Press in ½″ (1.3cm) deep pleats across the width of the strip, following the pleater manufacturer's directions. To secure the pleats, baste ⅜″ (1cm) from the long raw edges, as shown in **Diagram 7.**

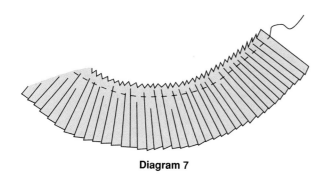

Diagram 7

4 Attaching the bias tape

Press under 1″ (2.5cm) on one end of two 50″ (127cm) long bias strips. Make single-fold bias tape from each strip, following the directions on page 125 for making single-fold bias tape.

⊕ DESIGN PLUS

To change the look of these place mats and shorten your sewing time, match the pleated portion of the trim to the place mat front. Substitute purchased 1″ (2.5cm) wide single-fold bias tape for the custom-made bias tape. For four place mats, you will need 11 yards (10.2m) of single-fold bias tape.

Unfold one long edge of one strip of bias tape. With right sides together, pin the tape to the long raw edge of the pleated trim, matching the unfolded long edge of the tape to the edge of the trim and the folded end of the trim to the folded end of the tape. Repeat, pinning the other strip of bias tape to the wrong side of the trim. Beginning ½″ (1.3cm) from the folded end, stitch ½″ (1.3cm) from the long raw edges, through all of the layers, as shown in **Diagram 8.**

½″ (1.3cm)

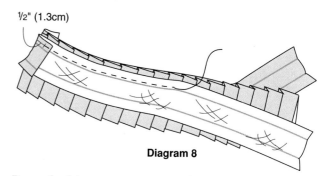

Diagram 8

Press the bias tapes up, away from the pleats. Trim the raw ends of the bias tape to match the raw ends of the pleats.

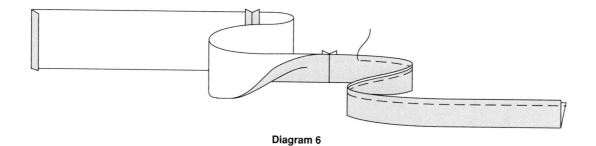

Diagram 6

5 Attaching the trim

Referring to **Diagram 9,** pin the trim to the place mat, encasing the edge of the place mat between the two strips of bias tape and lapping the folded ends of the pleats and the bias tapes over the cut ends of the pleats and the bias tapes. If necessary, trim the underlap to ½" (1.3cm).

Hold your steam iron a few inches above the binding and apply a generous amount of steam, shrinking the bias tape until it fits smoothly around the curve of the place mat. Turn the place mat over and repeat for the other side of the trim. Let the place mat dry thoroughly.

Using the fabric glue, glue the bias tapes to the place mat front and the place mat back, following the fabric glue manufacturer's directions. Glue the underlapping pleats to the inside of the overlapping pleats. Let the glue dry thoroughly.

On the right side of the place mat, stitch along both long edges of the binding, through all of the layers, as shown in **Diagram 10.**

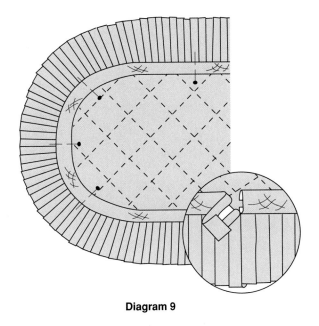

Diagram 9

Diagram 10

*When sunflowers are in bloom,
mornings can't be anything but sunny!*

SUNFLOWER SURPRISE

QUILTED PLACE MATS

Size:

Four 13″ × 19″ (33cm × 48.5cm) oval place mats

SUPPLIES

- *1⅞ yards (1.8m) of 45″ (115cm) wide cotton or cotton/polyester floral print fabric with approximately 3″ (7.5cm) diameter flowers*
- *½ yard (0.5m) of 45″ (115cm) wide cotton or cotton/polyester solid fabric*
- *¾ yard (0.7m) of 45″ (115cm) wide polyester batting*
- *Water-soluble marking pen*
- *Straight-edge ruler*
- *One 20″ × 26″ (51cm × 66cm) sheet of tissue paper*
- *Pencil*

CUTTING DIRECTIONS

Before cutting, review the information on page 123 for preshrinking fabric and trim.

Fold the tissue paper in half and then in quarters, matching the cut edges. Crease the folds. Unfold the tissue paper. Using the tissue paper and **Diagram 1** on page 60, match the tissue paper folds to the fold lines on the diagram. Using the pencil, trace the place mat cutting line onto the tissue paper, as shown in **Diagram 2.** Refold the tissue paper and cut along the marked line, through all of the layers of paper. Unfold the paper pattern.

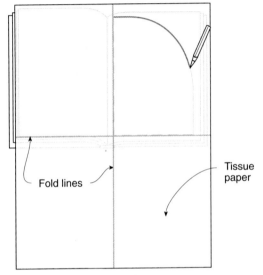

Fold lines

Tissue paper

Diagram 2

From the print fabric, cut eight 15″ × 21″ (38cm × 53.5cm) rectangles—four place mat fronts and four place mat backs.

From the solid fabric, cut 8 yards (7.4m) of 2″ (5cm) wide bias strips, following the directions on page 125 for making continuous bias strips. Cut the bias strip into four 60″ (153cm) lengths.

From the batting, cut four 15″ × 21″ (38cm × 53.5cm) batting sections.

⊕ DESIGN PLUS

Choose a solid fabric for the place mats. Replace the straight-stitch quilting with rows of decorative stitching. To emphasize the stitches, use rayon or metallic machine embroidery thread in the needle.

Diagram 1

Note: Pattern shown is actual size.

Place on fold

Place on fold

SEWING DIRECTIONS

Follow these directions for each place mat.

1 Marking the quilting lines

With right sides together, fold down one corner of one place mat front until the adjacent lengthwise and crosswise edges meet, as shown in **Diagram 3.** Press along the fold. Unfold the place mat front. Using the marking pen, mark the fold. Using the ruler and marking pen, draw a parallel line 2½″ (6.3cm) from the first line.

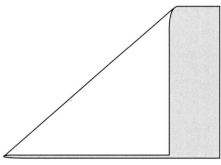

Diagram 3

Repeat, covering the place mat front with parallel lines that are 2½″ (6.3cm) apart. Repeat, folding down an adjacent corner, as shown in **Diagram 4,** and then drawing parallel lines that intersect with the first set of diagonal lines.

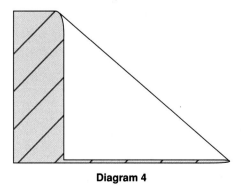

Diagram 4

2 Quilting the place mat

Working on a large, flat surface, lay one place mat back wrong side up. Place one batting section on top of the place mat back. Lay one place mat front,

right side up, over the batting. Pin the layers together at frequent intervals. Set the sewing machine stitch length for eight to ten stitches per inch (2.5cm). Machine stitch along the marked lines, through all of the layers, as shown in **Diagram 5.**

Diagram 5

Center the paper pattern over the quilted place mat. Trim the edges of the place mat to match the paper pattern.

3 Finishing the place mat

Make double-fold bias tape from one 60″ (153cm) long bias strip, following the directions on page 125 for making double-fold bias tape. Apply the tape to the edge of the place mat, as shown in the photograph on page 58 and following the directions on page 125 for applying double-fold bias tape.

🧵 SEW SIMPLE

Instead of marking and stitching parallel quilting lines, machine stitch around the dominant motifs in the fabric.

Ironing over marks made by some water-soluble marking pens can set them. If this happens, apply Spray and Wash Stain Stick to the marks and leave it on overnight. Launder according to the fabric's care requirements.

NAPKINS & NAPKIN RINGS

Size:

Four 18″ (45.5cm) square napkins and four napkin rings

SUPPLIES

- *1 yard (1m) of 45″ (115cm) wide cotton or cotton/polyester solid fabric*
- *¾ yard (0.7m) of 45″ (115cm) wide cotton or cotton/polyester floral print fabric with approximately 3″ (7.5cm) diameter flowers*
- *¼ yard (0.3m) of heavyweight fusible craft interfacing, such as Crafter's Choice or Pellon Decor-Bond*
- *¼ yard (0.3m) of paper-backed fusible web*
- *Small, sharp scissors*

CUTTING DIRECTIONS

Before cutting, review the information on page 123 for preshrinking fabric and trim.

All measurements include ½″ (1.3cm) seam allowances.

From the solid fabric, cut:

- *Four 18″ (45.5cm) square napkins*
- *Four 5″ × 7″ (12.5cm × 18cm) napkin rings*
- *Four 4″ (10cm) diameter circles*

From the floral print fabric, cut:

- *Four 4″ (10cm) diameter circles with 3″ (7.5cm) diameter flowers in the centers*
- *9 yards (8.4m) of 2″ (5cm) wide bias strips, following the directions on page 125 for making continuous bias strips. Cut the bias strip into four 78″ (199cm) lengths.*

From the fusible interfacing, cut:

- *Four 3¾″ (9.5cm) diameter circles*
- *Four 4″ × 6″ (10cm × 15cm) rectangles*

From the paper-backed fusible web, cut:

- *Four 3¾″ (9.5cm) diameter circles*
- *Four 2″ × 3½″ (5cm × 9cm) rectangles*

SEWING DIRECTIONS

Follow these directions for each napkin and napkin ring.

1 Making the napkin

Make double-fold bias tape from one 78″ (199cm) long bias strip, following the directions on page 125 for making double-fold bias tape. Apply the tape to the edges of one napkin, as shown in the photograph on page 58 and following the directions on page 125 for applying double-fold bias tape.

2 Making the napkin ring

Referring to **Diagram 1,** center one rectangle of fusible interfacing on the wrong side of one napkin ring rectangle. Fuse, following the fusible interfacing manufacturer's directions. Press under ½″ (1.3cm) on one end and then stitch.

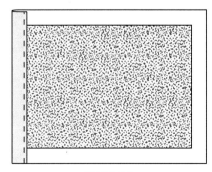

Diagram 1

Fold the rectangle in half lengthwise, with right sides together, and stitch the seam, as shown in **Diagram 2.** Trim the seam to ¼" (6mm) and press it open. Turn the rectangle right side out.

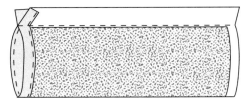

Diagram 2

Press so that the rectangle is flat and the seam is centered lengthwise on the rectangle, as shown in **Diagram 3.**

Diagram 3

Fuse one interfacing circle to the wrong side of one print fabric circle, following the fusible interfacing manufacturer's directions. Apply one fusible web circle to the wrong side of one solid fabric circle, following the fusible web manufacturer's directions. Peel off the paper backing. With wrong sides together, fuse the print fabric circle to the solid fabric circle, following the fusible web manufacturer's directions.

Place the circle, print side down, on a flat surface. Center the small rectangle of fusible web, paper side up, on the circle, as shown in **Diagram 4.**

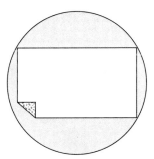

Diagram 4

Apply the fusible web, following the fusible web manufacturer's directions. Leave the paper backing in place. Turn the circle print side up. Using the small scissors, cut along the edges of the flower motif, as shown in **Diagram 5,** through all of the layers.

Diagram 5

Place the motif facedown on a flat surface. Peel off the paper backing. Center the napkin ring, seam side up, over the motif, as shown in **Diagram 6.** Fuse, following the fusible web manufacturer's directions.

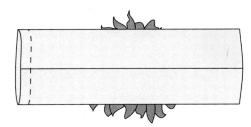

Diagram 6

Referring to **Diagram 7,** insert the cut end of the napkin ring into the hemmed end, forming a circle, and slip stitch, following the directions on page 124 for slip stitching.

Diagram 7

⊕ DESIGN PLUS

Assemble the floral motif as directed and glue it to a sturdy wood napkin ring, painted to coordinate with the fabric.

Re-create the look of yesteryear with quilted place mats in traditional American designs.

PIECED PATCHWORK

BASKET BLOCK PLACE MATS

Size:

Four 12″ × 18″ (30.5cm × 45.5cm) place mats

SUPPLIES

- *¾ yard (0.7m) of 45″ (115cm) wide cotton or cotton/polyester solid fabric*
- *1½ yards (1.4m) of 45″ (115cm) wide cotton or cotton/polyester blue print fabric*
- *¼ yard (0.3m) each of 45″ (115cm) wide cotton or cotton/polyester green and pink print fabric*
- *7 yards (6.5m) of ⅜″ (1cm) diameter piping cord*
- *1½ yards (1.4m) of 45″ (115cm) wide fusible fleece*
- *1 large sheet of tracing paper*
- *Soft lead pencil*
- *Water-soluble marking pen*

CUTTING DIRECTIONS

Before cutting, review the information on page 123 for preshrinking fabric and trim.

Using the tracing paper and pencil, trace the full-size patterns in **Diagrams 1, 2,** and **3** on pages 66 and 67 for the triangles, the handles, and the bow.

From the solid fabric, cut four 13″ × 19″ (33cm × 48.5cm) place mat fronts.

From the blue print fabric, cut:

- *Four 13″ × 19″ (33cm × 48.5cm) place mat backs*
- *20 triangle As, using the triangle pattern*
- *4 handles, using the handle pattern*
- *8 yards (7.4m) of 2″ (5cm) wide bias strips, following the directions on page 125 for making continuous bias strips. Cut the bias strips into four 65″ (165cm) lengths.*

From the green print fabric and using the triangle pattern, cut 24 triangle Bs.

From the pink print fabric and using the bow pattern, cut four bows.

From the fusible fleece, cut eight 13″ × 19″ (33cm × 48.5cm) batting sections.

Using the marking pen, mark the dots on the wrong sides of all of the triangles.

SEWING DIRECTIONS

Follow these directions for each place mat.

1 Preparing the front

Fuse one batting section to the wrong side of one place mat front, following the fusible fleece manufacturer's directions.

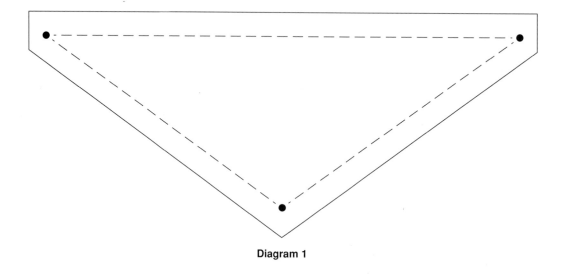

Diagram 1

Note: Patterns shown are actual size.

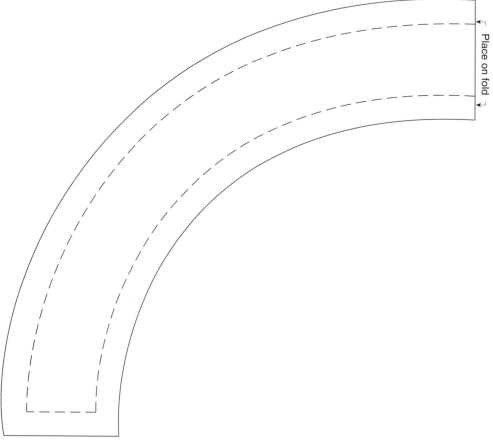

Place on fold

Diagram 2

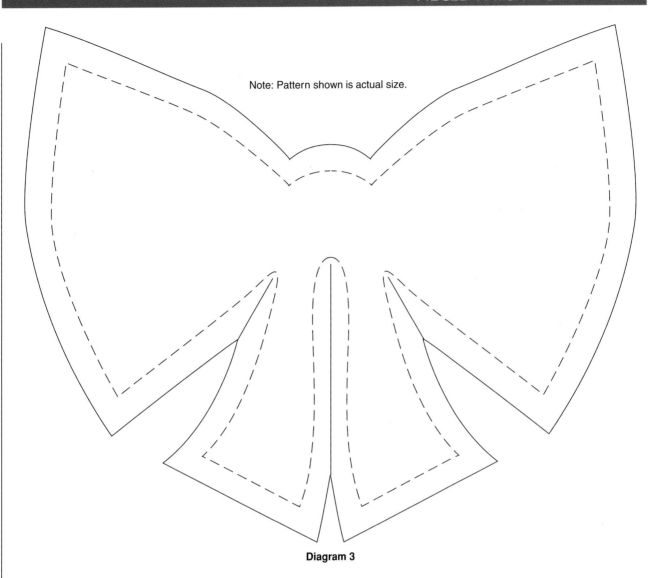

Note: Pattern shown is actual size.

Diagram 3

Make piping from one 65″ (165cm) long bias strip, following the directions on page 126 for making piping.

Referring to **Diagram 4** and working on the right side of the place mat front, machine baste the piping in place ½″ (1.3cm) from the raw edges, following the directions on page 126 for applying piping.

🧵 SEW SIMPLE

For faster sewing, use purchased piping. For four place mats, you will need 8 yards (7.4m) of piping. Eliminate the piping cord from the supply list and reduce the amount of blue print fabric to 1 yard (1m).

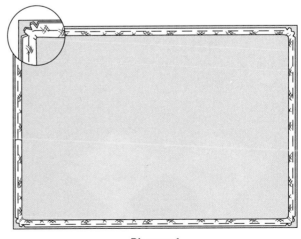

Diagram 4

2 Piecing the basket

With right sides together, using ¼″ (6mm) seams, and starting and ending the stitching at the dots, stitch one triangle A to two triangle Bs, as shown in **Diagram 5**. Press the seams to one side. This is the bottom row of the basket. Repeat, making the middle row of the basket.

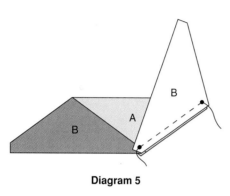

Diagram 5

With right sides together, using ¼″ (6mm) seams, and starting and ending the stitching at the dots, stitch three triangle As and two triangle Bs together and press the seams to one side, as shown in **Diagram 6**. This is the top row of the basket.

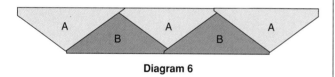

Diagram 6

With right sides together and using ¼″ (6mm) seams, stitch the three rows of triangles together and press the seams to one side, as shown in **Diagram 7**.

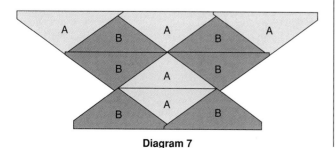

Diagram 7

3 Attaching the handle

Machine stitch ¼″ (6mm) from each curved edge of the handle and clip the curves, as shown in **Diagram 8**. Press under along the stitching lines.

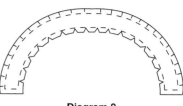

Diagram 8

With right sides together and raw edges matching, center and pin the handle to the upper edge of the basket. Machine stitch ¼″ (6mm) from the raw edges, as shown in **Diagram 9**. Press under ¼″ (6mm) on the upper edge of the basket, pressing the handle up.

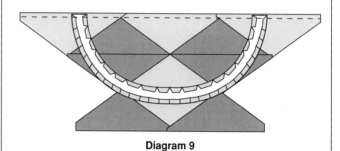

Diagram 9

Press under ¼″ (6mm) on the sides and lower edge of the basket.

Center the basket on the place mat front, as shown in the photograph on page 64, and slip stitch all around the edges, following the directions on page 124 for slip stitching.

Machine stitch along each seam where the triangles are joined.

4 Attaching the bow

Referring to **Diagram 10**, machine stitch ¼″ (6mm) from the edges of one bow and clip the curves. Press under along the stitching lines.

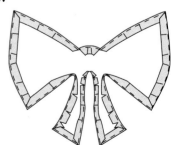

Diagram 10

Pin the bow over the basket handle, as shown in the photograph on page 64, and slip stitch all around the edges, following the directions on page 124 for slip stitching.

5 Finishing the place mat

Fuse one batting section to the wrong side of one place mat back, following the fusible fleece manufacturer's directions.

With right sides together, pin the place mat front to the place mat back. Using the sewing machine zipper foot attachment, stitch around the outer edge, crowding the stitches as close as possible to the piping cord and leaving an opening along one side edge that is large enough for turning, as shown

in **Diagram 11.** Trim the seam allowances to ¼″ (6mm) and clip the corners. Turn the place mat right side out. Slip stitch the opening closed, following the directions on page 124 for slip stitching.

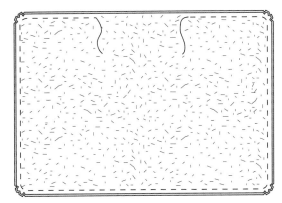

Diagram 11

SNOWFLAKE PLACE MATS

Size:

Four 12″ × 18″ (30.5cm × 45.5cm) place mats

SUPPLIES

- *1½ yards (1.4m) of 45″ (115cm) wide cotton or cotton/polyester print fabric*
- *½ yard (0.5m) of 45″ (115cm) wide cotton or cotton/polyester solid fabric*
- *7½ yards (6.9m) of jumbo rickrack*
- *1½ yards (1.4m) of 45″ (115cm) wide fusible fleece*
- *1 large sheet of tracing paper*
- *Soft lead pencil*

CUTTING DIRECTIONS

Before cutting, review the information on page 123 for preshrinking fabric and trim.

Using the tracing paper and pencil, trace the full-size patterns in **Diagrams 1** and **2** on page 70 for the triangles and the squares.

From the print fabric, cut:

- *Four 13″ × 19″ (33cm × 48.5cm) place mat fronts*
- *Four 13″ × 19″ (33cm × 48.5cm) place mat backs*

From the solid fabric and using the paper patterns, cut:

- *4 squares*
- *32 triangles*

From the fusible fleece, cut eight 13″ × 19″ (33cm × 48.5cm) batting sections.

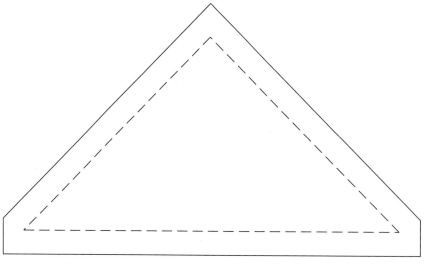

Diagram 1

Note: Patterns shown are actual size.

Diagram 2

SEWING DIRECTIONS

Follow these directions for each place mat.

1 Preparing the front

Fuse one batting section to the wrong side of one place mat front, following the fusible fleece manufacturer's directions.

Machine baste the rickrack in place ½" (1.3cm) from the raw edges of the place mat front, turning one rickrack end under and lapping it over the other end, as shown in **Diagram 3.**

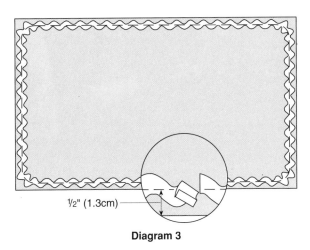

½" (1.3cm)

Diagram 3

2 Applying the snowflake

Press under ¼" (6mm) on the raw edges of one square and eight triangles.

Pin the square in place at the center of the place mat and pin two triangles on each side, forming a snowflake, as shown in the photograph on page 64. Slip stitch all around the edges, following the directions on page 124 for slip stitching.

3 Finishing the place mat

Fuse one batting section to the wrong side of one place mat back, following the fusible fleece manufacturer's directions.

With right sides together and the place mat front on top, pin the place mat front to the place mat back. Stitch around the outer edge, just inside the machine-basting stitches, leaving an opening along one side edge that is large enough for turning, as shown in **Diagram 4.** Trim the seam allowances to ¼" (6mm) and clip the corners, being careful not to cut the rickrack. Turn the place mat right side out. Slip stitch the opening closed, following the directions on page 124 for slip stitching.

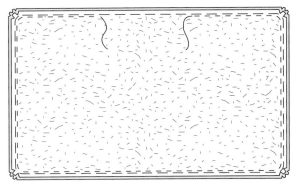

Diagram 4

🧵 SEW SIMPLE

After the raw edges of the squares and triangles are pressed under, apply paper-backed fusible web to the shapes. Peel off the paper backing; then arrange the square and the triangles on the place mat to form a snowflake. Fuse in place, following the fusible web manufacturer's directions. Finish the place mat, as in Step 3, and then machine quilt the snowflake, stitching just inside the edges of the square and the triangles.

Easy-sew ruffled seat covers paired wtih heart-shaped place mats add charm to the kitchen or breakfast nook.

HEARTS & FLOWERS

HEART PLACE MATS

Size:

Four 16″ × 17″ (40.5cm × 43cm) heart-shaped place mats

SUPPLIES

- *1½ yards (1.4m) of 45″ (115cm) wide cotton or cotton/polyester fabric*
- *7½ yards (6.9m) of contrasting covered piping*
- *1 yard (1m) of 45″ (115cm) wide polyester batting*
- *Tracing paper*
- *Soft lead pencil*

CUTTING DIRECTIONS

All measurements include ½″ (1.3cm) seam allowances.

Before cutting, review the information on page 123 for preshrinking fabric and trim.

Using the tracing paper and pencil, trace **Diagram 1.** Photocopy the traced pattern, enlarging it as indicated.

From the fabric and using the enlarged pattern, cut:

- *4 place mat fronts*
- *4 place mat backs*

From the batting and using the enlarged pattern, cut four batting sections.

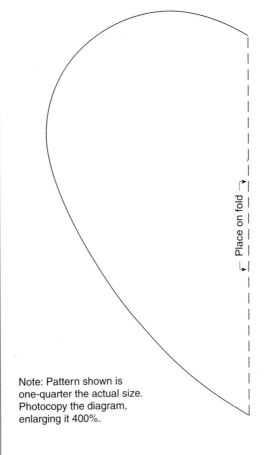

Note: Pattern shown is one-quarter the actual size. Photocopy the diagram, enlarging it 400%.

Place on fold

Diagram 1

🧵 SEW SIMPLE

Substitute fusible fleece for the polyester batting.

SEWING DIRECTIONS

Follow these directions for each place mat.

1 Preparing the front

Pin one batting section to the wrong side of one place mat front. Machine baste ⅜" (1cm) from the raw edges, as shown in **Diagram 2.**

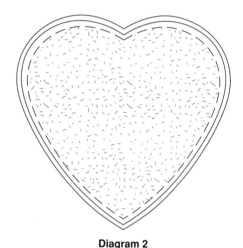

Diagram 2

Cut a 65" (165cm) length of piping. Referring to **Diagram 3** and working on the right side of the place mat front, machine baste the piping in place ½" (1.3cm) from the raw edges, following the directions on page 126 for applying piping.

Diagram 3

2 Assembling the place mat

With right sides together, pin the place mat front to the place mat back. Using the sewing machine zipper foot attachment, stitch around the outer edge, crowding the stitches as close as possible to the piping cord and leaving an opening along one side edge that is large enough for turning, as shown in **Diagram 4.** Trim the seam allowances to ¼" (6mm) and clip the corners. Turn the place mat right side out. Slip stitch the opening closed, following the directions on page 124 for slip stitching.

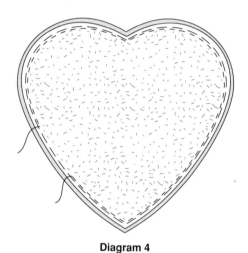

Diagram 4

✦ DESIGN PLUS

To add texture and interest, utilize the heart motif to machine quilt the place mat. Using an air-soluble marking pen, mark three or four concentric hearts, spaced 1" (2.5cm) apart, on the finished place mat. Machine stitch along the marked lines, through all of the layers. For an extra-special Valentine's Day celebration, consider red fabric, with white piping and white machine quilting.

Size:

To fit a chair with a seat that is approximately 17″ to 19″ × 17″ to 20″ (43cm to 48.5cm × 43cm to 51cm)

SUPPLIES

- *2⅛ yards (2m) of 45″ (115cm) or 54″ (138cm) wide decorator fabric, such as chintz or polished cotton*
- *½ yard (0.5m) of 45″ (115cm) wide contrasting fabric*
- *2½ yards (2.3m) of ⅜″ (1cm) diameter piping cord*
- *⅝ yard (0.6m) of 45″ (115cm) wide polyester batting*
- *1 yard (1m) of 45″ (115cm) wide muslin fabric*
- *Soft lead pencil*

CUTTING DIRECTIONS

All measurements include ½″ (1.3cm) seam allowances.

Before cutting, review the information on page 123 for preshrinking fabric and trim.

Referring to **Diagram 1,** cover the chair seat with the muslin. Using the pencil, trace the outer edge of the seat, tracing around the posts. Remove the muslin. Add a ½″ (1.3cm) seam allowance all around. Cut out the muslin pattern.

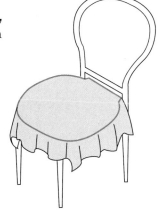

Diagram 1

From the decorator fabric, cut:

- *1 cover top, using the muslin pattern*
- *1 cover lining, using the muslin pattern*
- *Four 4½″ × 26″ (11.5cm × 66cm) ties*
- *Three 9″ × 45″ (23cm × 115cm) front ruffle sections*
- *One 9″ × 45″ (23cm × 115cm) back ruffle*

From the contrasting fabric, cut 8 yards (7.4m) of 2″ (5cm) wide bias strips, following the directions on page 125 for making continuous bias strips.

From the batting and using the muslin pattern, cut one batting section.

SEWING DIRECTIONS

1 Preparing the cover top

Pin the batting section to the wrong side of the cover top. Machine baste ⅜″ (1cm) from the raw edges, as shown in **Diagram 2.**

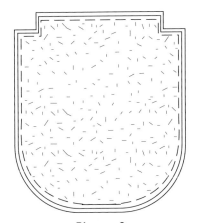

Diagram 2

Measure the outline of the seat on the muslin pattern and add 5″ (12.5cm). Cut a length of the bias strip equal to this measurement. Using this strip and the piping cord, make piping, following the directions on page 126 for making piping.

Referring to **Diagram 3** and working on the right side of the cover top, machine baste the piping in place ½″ (1.3cm) from the raw edges, along all of the edges, omitting the back corners.

Diagram 3

2 **Assembling the ties**

Referring to **Diagram 4,** fold one tie in half lengthwise, with right sides together, and pin. Measure and mark along the cut edge 1½″ (3.8cm) from one side edge. Draw a line from this mark to the diagonally opposite corner. Cut along this line.

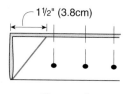

1½″ (3.8cm)

Diagram 4

Stitch ½″ (1.3cm) from the long cut edge and the diagonal cut edge, through both layers, as shown in **Diagram 5.** Turn the tie right side out and press. Press a 1½″ (3.8cm) pleat at the unstitched end and machine baste ⅜″ (1cm) from the raw edge.

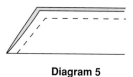

Diagram 5

Repeat, making three more ties.

Machine baste the ties to the right side of the cover top, as shown in **Diagram 6.** Place two ties at the back, ⅝″ (1.5cm) from the side edges, and place one tie on each side, ⅝″ (1.5cm) from the back edge.

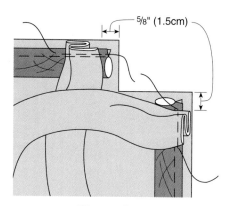

⅝″ (1.5cm)

Diagram 6

🧵 SEW SIMPLE

For faster sewing, use purchased piping, extra-wide double-fold bias tape, and ribbon ties.

- *To determine how much piping to purchase, measure the seat outline on the muslin pattern and add 5″ (12.5cm).*

- *To finish the edges of the ruffles, purchase 6¼ yards (5.8m) of extra-wide double-fold bias tape.*

- *For the ties, purchase 3 yards (2.8m) of 1½″ (39mm) wide ribbon.*

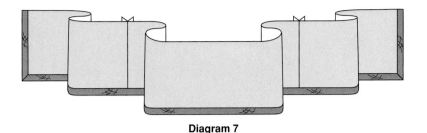

Diagram 7

3 Preparing the ruffles

With right sides together, stitch the front ruffle sections together at the ends to form one long ruffle. Press the seams open.

Make double-fold bias tape from the remaining bias strip, following the directions on page 125 for making double-fold bias tape.

Referring to **Diagram 7,** apply the double-fold bias tape to the ends and the lower edge of the front ruffle, following the directions on page 125 for applying double-fold bias tape. Repeat, applying the remaining double-fold bias tape to the back ruffle.

Machine baste along the raw edge of each ruffle, following the directions on page 124 for preparing a ruffle.

4 Attaching the ruffles

Referring to **Diagram 8,** with right sides together and the raw edges matching, stitch the ruffle to the

Diagram 8

front of the cover top and the back ruffle to the back of the cover top, matching the ends of the ruffles to the sides of the ties and following the directions on page 124 for gathering and attaching a ruffle.

5 Finishing the cover

With right sides together, pin the lining to the cover top. Using the sewing machine zipper foot attachment, stitch around the outer edge, crowding the stitches as close as possible to the piping cord and leaving an opening along the back edge large enough for turning, as shown in **Diagram 9.** Be careful not to catch the free ends of the ties in the stitching. Trim the seam allowances to ¼" (6mm) and clip the corners. Turn the cover right side out. Slip stitch the opening closed, following the directions on page 124 for slip stitching.

Diagram 9

INSTALLATION

Install the seat cover on the chair, as shown in the photograph on page 72.

Coordinating table runner, place mats, and napkins offer a new perspective on patchwork.

FOLDED PATCHWORK

PLACE MAT

Size:

One 12″ × 18½″ (30.5cm × 47cm) place mat

CUTTING DIRECTIONS

Before cutting, review the information on page 123 for preshrinking fabric and trim.

From the print fabric, cut:

- One 12″ × 18½″ (30.5cm × 47cm) place mat front
- One 12″ × 18½″ (30.5cm × 47cm) place mat back

From the solid fabric, cut:

- One 1½″ × 12″ (3.8cm × 30.5cm) sashing strip
- Two 1¾″ × 3½″ (4.5cm × 9cm) sashing strips
- 2 yards (1.9m) of 2″ (5cm) wide bias strips, following the directions on page 125 for making continuous bias strips

From the solid and the print fabrics, cut sections A through P, as indicated in the Patchwork Assembly Chart on page 80. Using the spray starch, starch and press sections A, G, and M flat. With wrong sides together, fold sections B through F, H through L, and N through P, as indicated in the chart; using the spray starch, starch and press the sections.

From the batting, cut one 12″ × 18½″ (30.5cm × 47cm) batting section.

🧵 SEW SIMPLE

Save sewing time by choosing a print fabric that is also available in a prequilted version. Purchase ⅜ yard (0.4m) of the print fabric for the patchwork squares and ⅜ yard (0.4m) of the prequilted version for the place mat front and place mat back. Eliminate the polyester batting. Follow the directions for the place mat. In Step 4, instead of quilting the place mat, put the place mat front and the place mat back wrong sides together and machine baste ⅜″ (1cm) from the cut edges, through all of the layers.

PATCHWORK ASSEMBLY CHART					
SQUARE	**SECTION**	**NUMBER TO CUT**	**SIZE**	**FABRIC**	**FOLD**
Gentleman's Fancy	A	1	3½″ (9cm) square	Print	—
	B	4	2½″ × 3½″ (6.3cm × 9cm)	Solid	Lengthwise
	C	4	2½″ (6.3cm) square	Print	Diagonally
	D	4	1½″ × 3½″ (3.8cm × 9cm)	Solid	Lengthwise
	E	4	1½″ (3.8cm) square	Print	Diagonally
	F	4	2″ (5cm) square	Print	Diagonally, then in half
Hole in the Barn Door	G	1	3½″ (9cm) square	Solid	—
	H	4	2¾″ (7cm) square	Print	Diagonally
	I	4	2″ × 3½″ (5cm × 9cm)	Solid	Lengthwise
	J	4	1⅛″ × 3½″ (2.8cm × 9cm)	Print	Lengthwise
	K	4	2″ (5cm) square	Solid	Lengthwise, then crosswise
	L	4	1¼″ (3.2cm) square	Print	Diagonally
Nine Patch	M	1	3½″ (9cm) square	Solid	—
	N	4	2⅞″ (7.3cm) square	Print	Diagonally
	O	4	3″ (7.5cm) square	Solid	Diagonally, then in half
	P	4	2″ (5cm) square	Print	Diagonally

SEWING DIRECTIONS

1 Assembling the Gentleman's Fancy folded square

With the cut edges matching, use the glue stick to baste the section Bs to the right side of section A, overlapping the sections, as shown in **Diagram 1.**

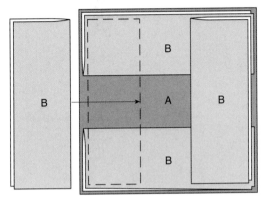

Diagram 1

Overlap and baste the section Cs, as shown in **Diagram 2.**

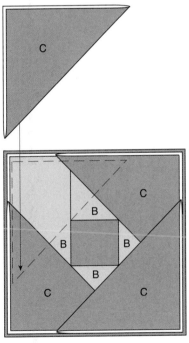

Diagram 2

Overlap and baste the section Ds, as shown in **Diagram 3.**

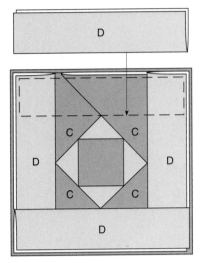

Diagram 3

Overlap and baste the section Es, as shown in **Diagram 4.**

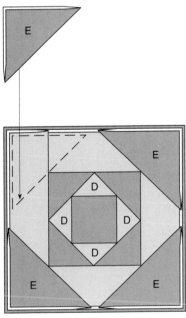

Diagram 4

Referring to **Diagram 5,** overlap and baste the section Fs. Press the square flat. Stitch all around the square ⅛″ (3mm) from the cut edges.

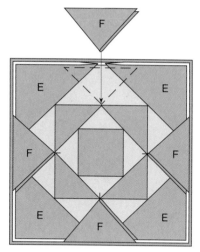

Diagram 5

Secure the point of each section F with a small hand stitch, as shown in **Diagram 6.**

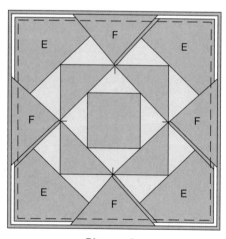

Diagram 6

2 Assembling the Hole in the Barn Door folded square

With the cut edges matching, use the glue stick to baste the section Hs to the right side of section G, as shown in **Diagram 7.**

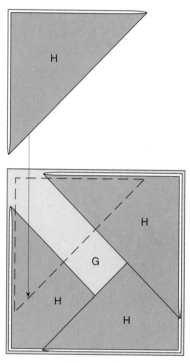

Diagram 7

Overlap and baste the section Is, as shown in **Diagram 8.**

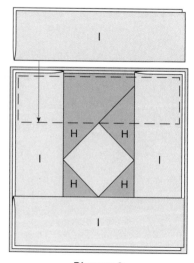

Diagram 8

Overlap and baste the section Js, as shown in **Diagram 9.**

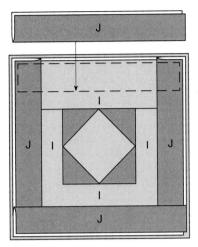

Diagram 9

Overlap and baste the section Ks, as shown in **Diagram 10.**

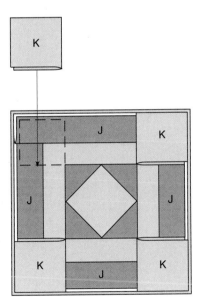

Diagram 10

Referring to **Diagram 11,** overlap and baste the section Ls. Press the square flat. Stitch all around the square ⅛″ (3mm) from the cut edges.

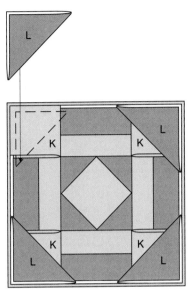

Diagram 11

Secure the point of each section K with a small hand stitch, as shown in **Diagram 12.**

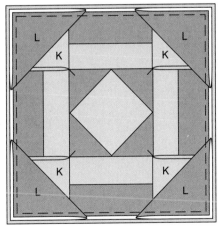

Diagram 12

3 Assembling the Nine Patch folded square

With the cut edges matching, use the glue stick to baste the section Ns to the right side of section M, overlapping the sections, as shown in **Diagram 13**.

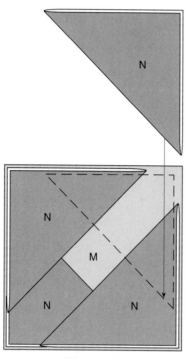

Diagram 13

Overlap and baste the section Os, as shown in **Diagram 14**.

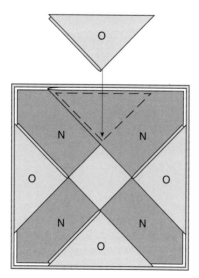

Diagram 14

Referring to **Diagram 15**, overlap and baste the section Ps. Press the square flat. Stitch all around the square ⅛″ (3mm) from the cut edges.

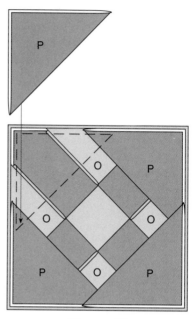

Diagram 15

Secure the point of each section O with a small hand stitch, as shown in **Diagram 16**.

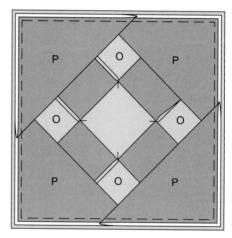

Diagram 16

4 Quilting the place mat

With right sides together, fold down one corner of the place mat front until the adjacent lengthwise and crosswise edges meet, as shown in **Diagram 17**.

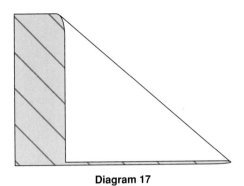

Diagram 17

Press along the fold. Unfold the place mat front. Using the marking pen, mark the fold. Using the ruler and marking pen, draw a parallel line 1⅛″ (2.8cm) from the first line. Repeat, covering the place mat front with parallel lines that are 1⅛″ (2.8cm) apart.

Working on a large, flat surface, lay the place mat back wrong side up. Lay the batting section on top of the place mat back. Lay the place mat front, right side up, over the batting. Pin the layers together at frequent intervals. Set the sewing machine stitch length for eight to ten stitches per inch (2.5cm). Machine stitch along the marked lines, through all of the layers, as shown in **Diagram 18**.

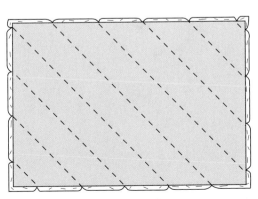

Diagram 18

SEW SIMPLE

Follow these tips for smooth, even machine quilting:

- *If tucks or puckers occur as you are quilting the place mat, or the layers do not feed evenly through the sewing machine, reduce the pressure on the sewing machine presser foot.*

- *Stitch all of the rows of quilting in the same direction.*

- *Use straight pins with large, round, plastic or glass heads. They will be more visible and easier to remove during stitching.*

5 Applying the squares

With the cut edges matching and using the glue stick, baste the Gentleman's Fancy square in place at the upper right corner of the place mat front. Baste the Nine Patch square in place at the lower right corner. Center the Hole in the Barn Door square between the other two squares and baste in place.

Press under ¼″ (6mm) on the long edges of all of the sashing strips.

Referring to **Diagram 19** on page 86 and using the glue stick, center and baste one short sashing strip over each space between the squares, matching the end of each strip to the cut edge of the place mat. Baste the long sashing strip along the inner edge of the squares so that the folded edge of the strip overlaps the squares by ¼″ (6mm). Slip stitch the strips in place along the pressed edges, following the directions on page 124 for slip stitching.

6 Binding the place mat

Make double-fold bias tape from the continuous bias strip, following the directions on page 125 for making double-fold bias tape. Apply the tape to the edge of the place mat, as shown in the photograph on page 78 and following the directions on page 125 for applying double-fold bias tape.

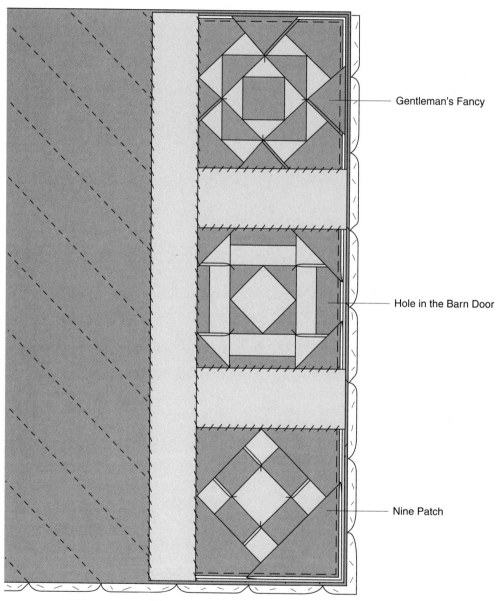

Diagram 19

NAPKIN

Size:

One 14½″ (37cm) square napkin

SUPPLIES

- *½ yard (0.5m) of 45″ (115cm) wide cotton or cotton/polyester solid fabric*
- *⅛ yard (0.2m) of 45″ (115cm) wide cotton or cotton/polyester print fabric*
- *Spray starch*
- *Glue stick*

CUTTING DIRECTIONS

Before cutting, review the information on page 123 for preshrinking fabric and trim.

From the solid fabric, cut:

- *One 15½″ (39.5cm) square napkin*
- *One 4⅛″ (10.5cm) square foundation*

From the solid and the print fabrics, cut sections A through F, as indicated in the Patchwork Assembly Chart on page 80. Using the spray starch, starch and press section A flat. With wrong sides together, fold sections B through F, as indicated in the chart; using the spray starch, starch and press the sections.

SEWING DIRECTIONS

1 Assembling the Gentleman's Fancy folded square

Following Step 1 on page 81, assemble the Gentleman's Fancy folded square.

2 Binding the square

Referring to **Diagram 1,** place the Gentleman's Fancy square right side up on the wrong side of the foundation so that two adjacent edges of the square match two adjacent edges of the foundation. Using the glue stick, baste the square in place. To form the binding, press down ½″ (1.3cm) on one extended edge of the foundation; tuck the raw edge in to meet the crease; press again. Slip stitch along the second fold, following the directions on page 124 for slip stitching.

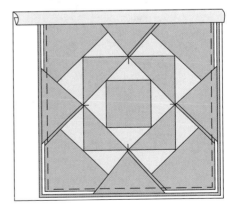

Diagram 1

Referring to **Diagram 2,** repeat, using the remaining extended edge of the foundation to bind the corresponding edge of the square.

Diagram 2

3 Finishing the napkin

Press up ¹/₂″ (1.3cm) on two opposite edges of the napkin. Tuck the raw edge in to meet the crease. Press again. Repeat for the remaining edges of the napkin.

Referring to **Diagram 3,** measure and mark two adjacent edges, 3¾″ (9.5cm) from one corner. Set the sewing machine for a blind hem stitch or a medium-length, medium-width zigzag stitch.

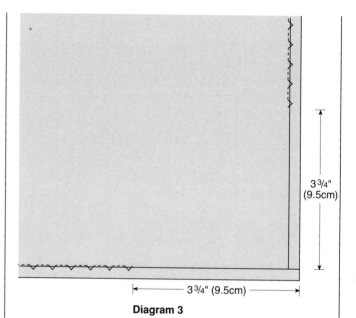

3¾″ (9.5cm)

3¾″ (9.5cm)

Diagram 3

Starting at one mark, stitch around the napkin along the inner hem fold, leaving the hem open at the corner between the marks.

Referring to the photograph on page 78, slip the cut edges of the folded square under the open hem allowance at the corner of the napkin. Slip stitch the hem allowance to the folded square and the bound edge of the folded square to the napkin, following the directions on page 124 for slip stitching.

TABLE RUNNER

Size:

12" × 48" (30.5cm × 122cm) table runner

SUPPLIES

- *2¼ yards (2.1m) of 45" (115cm) wide cotton or cotton/polyester print fabric*
- *1¾ yards (1.7m) of 45" (115cm) wide cotton or cotton/polyester solid fabric*
- *1⅜ yards (1.3m) of 45" (115cm) wide polyester batting*
- *Spray starch*
- *Glue stick*
- *Water-soluble marking pen*
- *Straight-edge ruler*

CUTTING DIRECTIONS

Before cutting, review the information on page 123 for preshrinking fabric and trim.

From the print fabric, cut:

- *One 12" × 35" (30.5cm × 89cm) front center panel*
- *One 12" × 35" (30.5cm × 89cm) back center panel*
- *Two 7½" × 12" (19cm × 30.5cm) front side panels*
- *Two 7½" × 12" (19cm × 30.5cm) back side panels*

From the solid fabric, cut:

- *Four 1½" × 12" (3.8cm × 30.5cm) sashing strips*
- *Four 1¾" × 3½" (4.5cm × 9cm) sashing strips*
- *3½ yards (3.3m) of 2" (5cm) wide bias strips, following the directions on page 125 for making continuous bias strips*

From the solid and the print fabrics, cut sections A through P, as indicated in the Patchwork Assembly Chart on page 80. Repeat, cutting a second set of sections A through P. Using the spray starch, starch and press sections A, G, and M flat. With wrong sides together, fold sections B through F, H through L, and N through P, as indicated in the chart; using the spray starch, starch and press the sections.

From the batting, cut one 12" × 48" (30.5cm × 122cm) batting section.

SEWING DIRECTIONS

1 Assembling the folded squares

Following Step 1 on page 81, assemble a Gentleman's Fancy folded square. Repeat, assembling a second Gentleman's Fancy folded square.

Following Step 2 on page 82, assemble a Hole in the Barn Door folded square. Repeat, assembling a second Hole in the Barn Door folded square.

Following Step 3 on page 84, assemble a Nine Patch folded square. Repeat, assembling a second Nine Patch folded square.

2 Preparing the table runner sections

With right sides together, stitch one front side panel to each side edge of the front center panel, as shown in **Diagram 1**, stitching ½" (1.3cm) from the cut edges. Press the seams open.

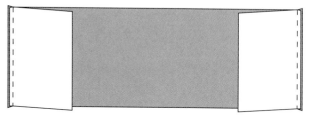

Diagram 1

Repeat, stitching one back side panel to each side edge of the back center panel.

3 Quilting the table runner

With right sides together, fold down one corner of the table runner front until adjacent lengthwise and crosswise edges meet, as shown in **Diagram 2.** Press along the fold. Unfold the table runner front. Using the marking pen, mark the fold. Using the ruler and marking pen, draw a parallel line 1⅛" (2.8cm) from the first line. Repeat, covering the table runner front with parallel lines that are 1⅛" (2.8cm) apart.

Diagram 2

Working on a large, flat surface, place the table runner back wrong side up. Place the batting section on top of the table runner back. Place the table runner front, right side up, over the batting. Pin the layers together at frequent intervals. Set the sewing machine stitch length for eight to ten

stitches per inch (2.5cm). Machine stitch along the marked lines, through all of the layers, as shown in **Diagram 3.**

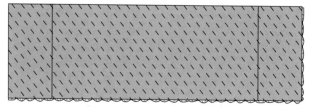

Diagram 3

4 Applying the squares

Press under ¼" (6mm) on the long edges of all of the sashing strips.

Using the glue stick and referring to **Diagram 4**, baste one Gentleman's Fancy square in place at the upper right edge of the table runner, matching the outer edge of the square to the seam line on the right and the upper edge of the square to the edge of the table runner.

Baste one Nine Patch square in place at the lower right edge of the table runner, matching the outer edge of the square to the seam line and the lower edge of the square to the lower edge of the table runner. Center one Hole in the Barn Door square between the other two squares, matching the outer edge of the square to the seam line. Repeat, basting the remaining folded squares so that they are aligned with the seam line at the other end of the table runner.

Referring to the photograph on page 78 and using the glue stick, center and baste one short sashing strip over each space between the squares on one end of the table runner. Baste one long sashing strip along the inner edge of the squares so that the folded edge of the strip overlaps onto the squares by ¼" (6mm). Repeat, basting one vertical sashing strip along the outer edge of the squares. Slip stitch the strips in place along the pressed edges, following the directions on page 124 for slip stitching. Repeat, applying the remaining sashing strips to the other end of the table runner.

Diagram 4

5 Finishing the table runner

Make double-fold bias tape from the continuous bias strip, following the directions on page 125 for making double-fold bias tape. Apply the tape to the edge of the place mat, as shown in the photograph on page 78 and following the directions on page 125 for applying double-fold bias tape.

When scrap-bag treasures get a new lease on life,
it's patch as patch can!

QUICK PATCH

Size:

Four 12″ × 18″ (30.5cm × 45.5cm) place mats and four 18″ (45.5cm) square napkins

SUPPLIES

- *1¾ yards (1.7m) of 45″ (115cm) wide cotton or cotton/polyester rose print fabric*
- *1 yard (1m) of 45″ (115cm) wide cotton or cotton/polyester mini-plaid fabric*
- *⅜ yard (0.4m) each of four 45″ (115cm) wide cotton or cotton/polyester coordinating print fabrics*
- *¾ yard (0.7m) of 45″ (115cm) wide polyester batting*

CUTTING DIRECTIONS

All measurements include ½″ (1.3cm) seam allowances.

Before cutting, review the information on page 123 for preshrinking fabric and trim.

From the rose print fabric, cut:

- *Four 12″ × 18″ (30.5cm × 45.5cm) place mat backs*
- *Four 18″ (45.5cm) square napkins*
- *Four 6″ × 7″ (15cm × 18cm) rectangle As*

From the mini-plaid fabric, cut:

- *16 yards (14.8m) of 2″ (5cm) wide bias strips, following the directions on page 125 for making continuous bias strips. From the bias strips, cut*

four 66″ (168cm) lengths and four 78″ (199cm) lengths.

- *Sixteen 3½″ × 4″ (9cm × 10cm) rectangle Bs*

From one coordinating print fabric, cut:

- *Eight 3½″ × 4″ (9cm × 10cm) rectangle Cs*
- *Four 2¼″ × 6″ (5.7cm × 15cm) rectangle Ds*

From the second coordinating print fabric, cut eight 4″ × 7″ (10cm × 18cm) rectangle Es.

From the third coordinating print fabric, cut:

- *Eight 4″ × 7″ (10cm × 18cm) rectangle Fs*
- *Eight 2¼″ × 6″ (5.7cm × 15cm) rectangle Gs*

From the fourth coordinating fabric, cut:

- *Eight 3½″ × 4″ (9cm × 10cm) rectangle Hs*
- *Four 2¼″ × 6″ (5.7cm × 15cm) rectangle Is*

From the batting, cut four 12″ × 18″ (30.5cm × 45.5cm) batting sections.

✦ DESIGN PLUS

Transform these simple country place mats into a fancy Victorian table setting. Add washable taffeta and cotton velveteen to your fabric mix. Before assembling the rectangles, embellish them with machine embroidery, small appliqués, or bits of ribbon and lace.

SEWING DIRECTIONS

Follow these directions for each place mat and napkin.

1 Joining the side strips

Referring to **Diagram 1** and with right sides together, stitch one rectangle C to one rectangle B along one 3½″ (9cm) edge. Stitch one rectangle E to one rectangle F along one 7″ (18cm) edge. Stitch one rectangle H to one rectangle B along one 3½″ (9cm) edge. Trim the seam allowances to ¼″ (6mm) and press them open.

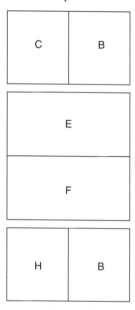

Diagram 1

Referring to **Diagram 2,** stitch the three pairs of rectangles together to form one 7″ × 12″ (18cm × 30.5cm) side strip. Trim the seam allowances to ¼″ (6mm) and press them open.

🧵 SEW SIMPLE

Using a water-soluble marking pen, mark the letter on the back of each rectangle. To speed up your sewing, assemble all of the place mat fronts and then complete each place mat.

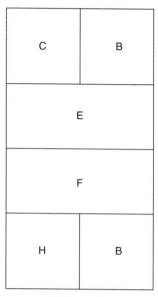

Diagram 2

Repeat, making another side strip.

2 Joining the center strip

Referring to **Diagram 3** and with right sides together, stitch one rectangle I to one 6″ (15cm) edge of one rectangle A. Stitch one rectangle D to the other 6″ (15cm) edge of rectangle A. Stitch one rectangle G to each 6″ (15cm) end of this strip. Trim the seam allowances to ¼″ (6mm) and press them open.

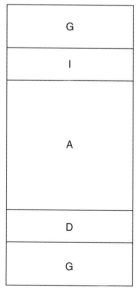

Diagram 3

3 Assembling the place mat front

Referring to **Diagram 4,** with right sides together, stitch one side strip to each long edge of the center strip, turning one side strip so that it is the reverse image of the other. Trim the seam allowances to ¼″ (6mm) and press them open.

C	B	G / I	B	H

(table representation of diagram 4)

Diagram 4

4 Quilting the place mat

Working on a large, flat surface, place one place mat back wrong side up. Lay one batting section on top of the place mat back. Lay one place mat front, right side up, over the batting. Pin the layers together at frequent intervals. Set the sewing machine stitch length for eight to ten stitches per inch (2.5cm). Machine stitch along the seam lines, through all of the layers, as shown in **Diagram 5.**

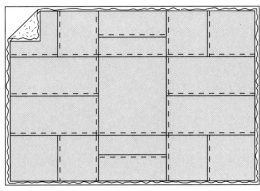

Diagram 5

5 Finishing the place mat

Make double-fold bias tape from one 66″ (168cm) long bias strip, following the directions on page 125 for making double-fold bias tape. Apply the tape to the edge of the place mat, as shown in the photograph on page 92 and following the directions on page 125 for applying double-fold bias tape.

6 Making the napkin

Make double-fold bias tape from one 78″ (199cm) long bias strip, following the directions on page 125 for making double-fold bias tape. Apply the tape to the edges of one napkin, as shown in the photograph on page 92 and following the directions on page 125 for applying double-fold bias tape.

A reversible table runner with one side printed, one side plain, gives your table two looks for the price of one.

Size:

One 16″ × 68″ (40.5cm × 173cm) table runner

SUPPLIES

- *2 yards (1.9m) of 45″ to 60″ (115cm to 153cm) wide print fabric*
- *2 yards (1.9m) of 45″ to 60″ (115cm to 153cm) wide solid fabric*
- *5 yards (4.6m) of ½″ (1.3cm) diameter twisted cord piping*
- *Two 3½″ (9cm) long tassels*
- *One 36″ (91.5cm) straight-edge ruler*
- *Water-soluble marking pen*
- *Seam ripper or small scissors*
- *Transparent tape*

CUTTING DIRECTIONS

All measurements include ½″ (1.3cm) seam allowances.

Before cutting, review the information on page 123 for preshrinking fabric and trim.

From the print fabric, cut one 17″ × 69″ (43cm × 176cm) runner front.

From the solid fabric, cut one 17″ × 69″ (43cm × 176cm) runner back.

Referring to **Diagram 1,** with right sides together, fold the runner front in half lengthwise. Pin the layers together at the raw edges. Using the ruler and marking pen and working on the long raw edge, measure in 9″ (23cm) from one side edge; mark. Draw a diagonal line from the mark to the nearest corner on the folded edge. Repeat for the other side edge. Cut along each line, through both layers of fabric. Remove the pins and unfold the front. Repeat for the back.

✿ DESIGN PLUS

Because the front and back of the runner are cut lengthwise, you will have enough fabric left over to make a second runner or an assortment of matching napkins. To make napkins, follow the directions on page 62.

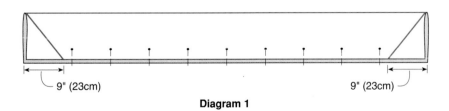

Diagram 1

SEWING DIRECTIONS

1 Preparing the front

Using the marking pen, make a mark at any point along one long edge on the right side of the runner front. Referring to **Diagram 2** and using the sewing machine zipper foot attachment, machine baste the piping in place ½″ (1.3cm) from the raw edges of the runner front, beginning and ending the basting 2″ (5cm) from the mark and leaving approximately 3″ (7.5cm) long tails.

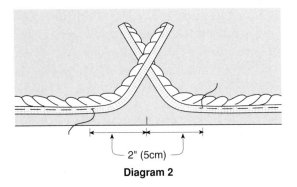

2″ (5cm)

Diagram 2

Using the seam ripper or small scissors, separate the lip from the cord on the tails. Referring to **Diagram 3,** separate the cords into plies and wrap each end with transparent tape. Trim each lip to 1″ (2.5cm), butt the ends together, and wrap them with tape.

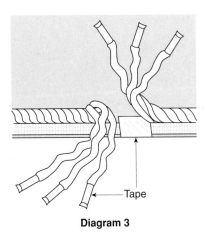

Tape

Diagram 3

Tuck the plies on the right tail behind the taped ends of the lips, as shown in **Diagram 4,** twisting and arranging the plies into their original shape. Secure with tape. Twist and arrange the plies on the left tail until the cord looks like one continuous piece.

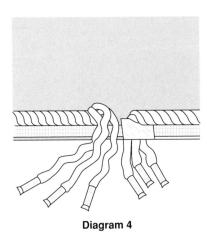

Diagram 4

Machine baste the ends of the piping in place, as shown in **Diagram 5.** Trim the tails of the plies to ½″ (1.3cm).

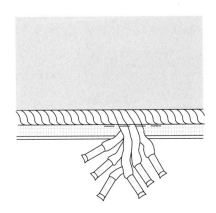

Diagram 5

🧵 SEW SIMPLE

To add body to your runner, apply fusible fleece to the wrong side of the front of the runner before basting the piping in place.

2 Assembling the runner

With right sides together, pin the runner front to the runner back. Using the sewing machine zipper foot attachment, stitch around the outer edge, crowding the stitches as close as possible to the cord and leaving an opening along one long edge that is large enough for turning, as shown in **Diagram 6.** Trim the corners on the diagonal.

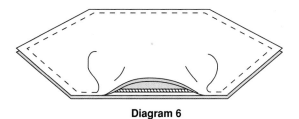

Diagram 6

Turn the runner right side out. Slip stitch the opening closed, following the directions on page 124 for slip stitching.

Hand sew a tassel to the point at each end of the runner.

✛ DESIGN PLUS

For a special occasion, choose opulent fabrics, such as brocade, cotton velveteen, moiré taffeta, or tapestry. Pay careful attention to the fabrics' care requirements. If you choose tassels that are not washable, use hooks and eyes to make them easy to remove. Sew a hook to the back of the runner at each point. Sew the corresponding eye to the top of the tassel.

*Give your furnishings a face-lift
with cheerful fabric accents.*

FABRIC FACE-LIFTS

RUFFLED PLACE MATS

Size:

Four 11″ × 17″ (28cm × 43cm) oval place mats, excluding the ruffle

SUPPLIES

- *3 yards (2.8m) of 45″ (115cm) wide cotton or cotton/polyester fabric*
- *¾ yard (0.7m) of 45″ (115cm) wide fusible fleece*
- *5⅝ yards (5.2m) of contrasting covered piping*
- *One 20″ × 26″ (51cm × 66cm) sheet of tissue paper*
- *Soft lead pencil*

CUTTING DIRECTIONS

Before cutting, review the information on page 123 for preshrinking fabric and trim.

Fold the tissue paper in half and then in quarters, matching the cut edges. Crease the folds. Unfold the tissue paper. Using the tissue paper and **Diagram 1** on page 54, match the tissue paper folds to the fold lines on the diagram. Using the pencil, trace the place mat cutting line onto the tissue paper, as shown in **Diagram 1.** Refold the tissue paper and cut along the marked line, through all of the layers of paper. Unfold the paper pattern.

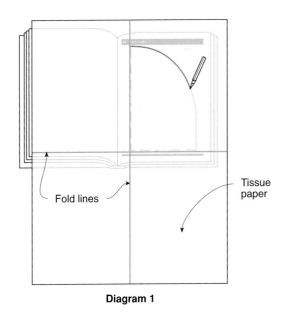

Fold lines

Tissue paper

Diagram 1

From the fabric, cut:

- *Four 13″ × 19″ (33cm × 48.5cm) place mat fronts*
- *Four 13″ × 19″ (33cm × 48.5cm) place mat backs*
- *Eight 5″ × 45″ (12.5cm × 115cm) ruffle sections*
- *Four 5″ × 22½″ (12.5cm × 57cm) ruffle sections*

From the fusible fleece, cut four 13″ × 19″ (33cm × 48.5cm) batting sections.

SEWING DIRECTIONS

Follow these directions for each place mat.

1 Preparing the front

Fuse one batting section to the wrong side of one place mat front, following the fusible fleece manufacturer's directions.

Cut a 50" (127cm) length of piping. Referring to **Diagram 2** and working on the right side of the place mat front, machine baste the piping in place ½" (1.3cm) from the raw edge, following the directions on page 126 for applying piping.

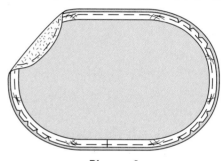

Diagram 2

Divide and mark the edge of the place mat front into eight equal parts.

2 Preparing and attaching the ruffle

Referring to **Diagram 3,** with right sides together, stitch two 45" (115cm) long ruffle sections and one 22½" (57cm) long ruffle section together at the ends to form one continuous ruffle. Press the seams open. With wrong sides together, fold the ruffle in half lengthwise and press. Machine baste along the raw edges, following the directions on page 124 for preparing a ruffle.

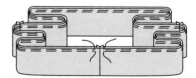

Diagram 3

Divide and mark the raw edge of the ruffle into eight equal parts.

Referring to **Diagram 4,** with right sides together, machine baste the ruffle to the place mat front, following the directions on page 124 for gathering and attaching a ruffle.

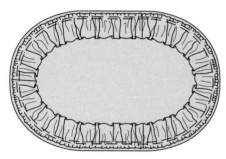

Diagram 4

3 Assembling the place mat

With right sides together, pin the place mat front to the place mat back. Using the sewing machine zipper foot attachment, stitch around the outer edge, crowding the stitches as close as possible to the piping cord and leaving an opening that is large enough for turning, as shown in **Diagram 5.** Trim the seam allowances to ¼" (6mm) and clip the curves. Turn the place mat right side out. Slip stitch the opening closed, following the directions on page 124 for slip stitching.

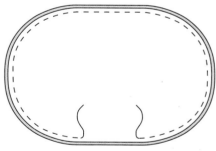

Diagram 5

🧵 SEW SIMPLE

Substitute pregathered trim for the fabric ruffle. For four place mats, purchase 5⅝ yards (5.2m) of 2" (5cm) wide pregathered trim and reduce the amount of fabric for the place mats to 1⅝ yards (1.5m).

Size:

To fit a chair with a seat that is approximately 13″ × 14″ (33cm × 35.5cm) and a back that is approximately 14″ × 21″ (35.5cm × 53.5cm)

SUPPLIES

- *1¾ yards (1.7m) of 54″ (138cm) wide cotton or cotton/polyester fabric*

- *1 yard (1m) of 45″ (115cm) wide muslin fabric*

- *½ yard (0.5m) of 45″ (115cm) wide fusible fleece*

- *5½″ (14cm) wide bullion fringe**

- *2¼ yards (2.1m) of ½″ (1.3cm) diameter twisted cord*

- *⅜″ (1cm) diameter piping cord**

- *1″ (2.5cm) thick foam**

- *Soft lead pencil*

- *Fabric glue, such as Aleene's OK to Wash It*

*See the "Cutting Directions" for additional information.

CUTTING DIRECTIONS

Before cutting, review the information on page 123 for preshrinking fabric and trim.

Measure the chair seat and the chair back. Then:

- *Purchase enough bullion fringe to equal the perimeter of the chair seat plus 1″ (2.5cm).*

- *Purchase enough piping cord to equal the perimeter of the chair back plus 2″ (5cm).*

- *Purchase a piece of 1″ (2.5cm) thick foam equal to the width × the length of the chair back.*

Referring to **Diagram 1,** center the muslin over the chair seat. Using the pencil, trace the edge of the seat. Mark the position of the back posts. Remove the muslin.

Diagram 1

Referring to **Diagram 2,** add 5″ (12.5cm) extensions to the front and side edges. Add a 5″ (12.5cm) extension to the back edge between the post markings. Add a ½″ (1.3cm) seam allowance all around.

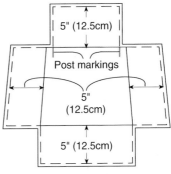

Diagram 2

From the cotton fabric and using the muslin seat pattern, cut:

- *1 seat cover front*

- *1 seat cover lining*

From the remaining cotton fabric, cut:

- *1 cushion cover front equal to the width × the length of the chair back plus ½″ (1.3cm) all around*

- *1 cushion cover back equal to the width × the length of the chair back plus ½" (1.3cm) all around*

- *Eight 1" × 14" (2.5cm × 35.5cm) ties*

- *2" (5cm) wide bias strips in an amount equal to the length of the piping cord, following the directions on page 125 for making continuous bias strips*

From the fusible fleece, cut two batting sections, each equal to the width × the length of the chair seat.

SEWING DIRECTIONS

1 Assembling the seat cover

Center one batting section on the wrong side of the seat cover front and fuse in place, following the fusible fleece manufacturer's directions. Repeat, fusing the other batting section to the seat cover lining.

With right sides together, stitch the seat cover front to the seat cover lining, leaving the front corners open, as shown in **Diagram 3.** Trim the seam allowances and trim the corners on the diagonal. Turn the cover right side out. Press the cover flat.

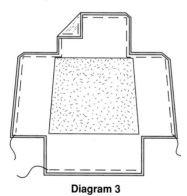

Diagram 3

🧵 SEW SIMPLE

If the seat cover extensions do not hang straight, sew small drapery weights to the lining at the corners, along the lower edges of the extensions.

Referring to **Diagram 4,** with right sides together, match the raw edges of one side extension to the corresponding raw edges of the front extension; stitch ½" (1.3cm) from the raw edges. Stitch again ¼" (6mm) from the raw edges. Trim the seam allowances close to the second row of stitches. Repeat, stitching the other front corner closed.

Diagram 4

2 Trimming the seat cover

Cut a piece of fringe equal to the length of the front and side extensions plus 1" (2.5cm). Referring to the photograph on page 100, center the seat cover on the chair seat. Pin the fringe to the upper edge of the side and front extensions, turning the ends of the fringe under ½" (1.3cm). Using the fabric glue, glue the fringe header to the cover. Repeat, gluing the fringe in place on the back extension.

Remove the cover from the chair. Cut the twisted cord into two equal lengths. Referring to **Diagram 5,** hand sew the center of one cord in place at one back corner of the seat cover. Tie a half-knot in each cord tail, about 3" (7.5cm) from the end of the cord. Separate the strands of the cord below the knot, forming a tassel. Repeat, attaching a tie to the other back corner.

Diagram 5

3 Making the cushion ties

With wrong sides together, press one 14″ (35.5cm) tie in half lengthwise. Unfold the tie. Referring to **Diagram 6,** press under ¼″ (6mm) on one short end and then fold both long edges in to meet the crease; press.

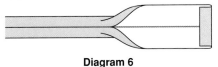

Diagram 6

Refold the tie along the first long crease. Press again. Referring to **Diagram 7,** stitch close to the folded edges, through all of the layers.

Diagram 7

Repeat, making seven more ties.

4 Preparing the cushion cover front

Using the continuous bias strip and the piping cord, make piping, following the directions on page 126 for making piping.

Referring to **Diagram 8** and working on the right side of the cushion cover front, machine baste the piping in place ½″ (1.3cm) from the raw edges, following the directions on page 126 for applying piping. As shown in Diagram 8, pin two ties at each corner so that each tie is ⅝″ (1.5cm) from the corner, with the end of the tie even with the raw edge of the cover front; machine baste in place.

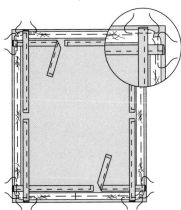

Diagram 8

5 Finishing the cushion

With right sides together, pin the cushion cover back to the cushion cover front. Using the sewing machine zipper foot attachment, stitch around the outer edge, crowding the stitches as close as possible to the piping cord and leaving a 10″ (25.5cm) opening along the lower edge for turning, as shown in **Diagram 9.** Be careful not to catch the free ends of the ties in the stitching. Trim the seam allowances to ¼″ (6mm) and trim the corners on the diagonal.

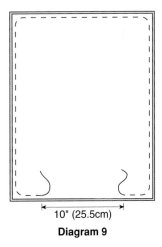

10″ (25.5cm)

Diagram 9

Turn the cover right side out. Insert the foam into the cover. Slip stitch the opening closed, following the directions on page 124 for slip stitching.

INSTALLATION

Install the seat cover on the seat and the cushion on the back of the chair, as shown in the photograph on page 100.

⊕ DESIGN PLUS

This cover and cushion combination is equally beautiful, although not washable, in a traditional upholstery fabric. For the cushion, substitute twisted cord piping for the fabric-covered piping and tasseled chair ties for the fabric ties.

STOOL COVER

Size:

To fit a stool with a 13″ (33cm) diameter seat

SUPPLIES

- *1½ yards (1.4m) of 45″ (115cm) wide cotton or cotton/polyester fabric*
- *1¼ yards (1.2m) of ⅜″ (1cm) diameter piping cord*
- *½ yard (0.5m) of 45″ (115cm) wide polyester batting*
- *15″ (38cm) square piece of brown paper*
- *Water-soluble marking pen*
- *Ruler*
- *Soft lead pencil*

CUTTING DIRECTIONS

All measurements include ½″ (1.3cm) seam allowances.

Before cutting, review the information on page 123 for preshrinking fabric and trim.

Turn the stool upside down and center it on the brown paper. Using the pencil, trace around the seat. Remove the stool. Add ½″ (1.3cm) to the edge of the outline.

From the fabric, cut:

- *1 cover top, using the paper pattern*
- *Three 9″ × 43″ (23cm × 110cm) skirt sections*
- *1¼ yards (1.2m) of 2″ (5cm) wide continuous bias strips, following the directions on page 125 for making continuous bias strips*

From the batting and using the paper pattern, cut one batting section.

SEWING DIRECTIONS

1 Preparing the cover top

Pin the batting to the wrong side of the cover top. Machine baste ⅜″ (1cm) from the raw edges, as shown in **Diagram 1.**

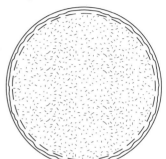

Diagram 1

Using the bias strips and the piping cord, make piping, following the directions on page 126 for making piping. Referring to **Diagram 2** and working on the right side of the cover top, machine baste the piping in place ½″ (1.3cm) from the raw edge, following the directions on page 126 for applying piping.

Diagram 2

2 Assembling the skirt

Referring to **Diagram 3,** stitch the three skirt sections together at the ends to form one long skirt section. Press the seams open. Press under ½″ (1.3cm) on one long edge. Tuck the raw edge in to meet the crease. Press again. Stitch close to the second fold.

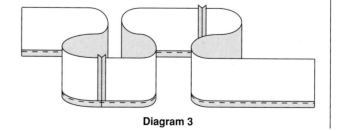

Diagram 3

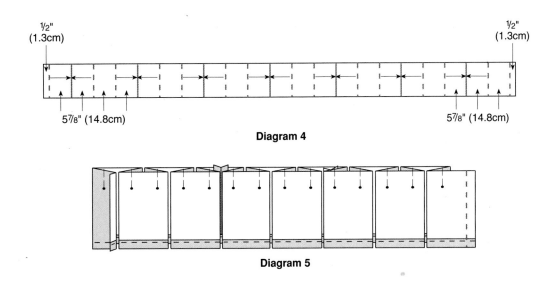

½"
(1.3cm)

½"
(1.3cm)

5⅞" (14.8cm)

5⅞" (14.8cm)

Diagram 4

Diagram 5

Referring to **Diagram 4,** using the ruler and marking pen, and working on the wrong side, measure and mark a broken line ½" (1.3cm) from the left end of the skirt. Beginning at the broken line, measure and mark lines that are 5⅞" (14.8cm) apart, alternating one solid and two broken lines seven times. Measure and mark a line ½" (1.3cm) beyond the last broken line; cut along this marked line, cutting off the excess fabric.

Form the pleats by folding and pressing along the broken lines and bringing them to meet the solid lines, as indicated in **Diagram 4**. Working on the right side, pin the pleats in place along the long raw edge, as shown in **Diagram 5.**

Referring to **Diagram 6,** with right sides together, stitch the ends of the skirt section together to form one continuous skirt. Press the seam open so that the seam allowances follow the fold.

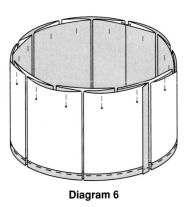

Diagram 6

3 Attaching the skirt

With the right sides together and raw edges matching, pin the skirt to the cover top. Using the sewing machine zipper foot attachment, stitch around the outer edge, crowding the stitches as close as possible to the piping cord, as shown in **Diagram 7.** Trim the seam allowances and clip along the curve.

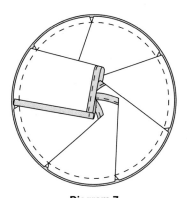

Diagram 7

INSTALLATION

Turn the stool cover right side out and position it over the stool seat, as shown in the photograph on page 100.

A clever twist transforms familiar napkin rings
into fashionable table accessories.

TWIST & TRIM

Size:

Four 18″ (45.5cm) square napkins and four napkin rings

SUPPLIES

- *1⅛ yards (1.1m) of 45″ (115cm) wide cotton or cotton/polyester print fabric*
- *½ yard (0.5m) of 45″ (115cm) wide cotton or cotton/polyester solid fabric*
- *8¼ yards (7.6m) of jumbo rickrack*
- *2 yards (1.9m) of ½″ (1.3cm) diameter piping cord*
- *Glue stick*
- *1 large safety pin*
- *Masking tape*
- *Strong string*

CUTTING DIRECTIONS

Before cutting, review the information on page 123 for preshrinking fabric and trim.

From the print fabric, cut four 19″ (48.5cm) square napkins.

From the solid fabric, cut four 3½″ (9cm) wide × 24″ (61cm) long bias strips.

SEWING DIRECTIONS

Follow these directions for each napkin and napkin ring.

1 Making the napkin

Referring to **Diagram 1,** press under ½″ (1.3cm) on two opposite edges of one napkin. Tuck each edge in to meet the crease. Press again. Stitch close to the second fold. Repeat for the remaining opposite edges.

Diagram 1

Referring to **Diagram 2** on page110, working on the right side of the napkin and using the glue stick, baste the rickrack in place around the napkin so that the outside scallops extend beyond the edge of the napkin and the cut ends of the rickrack are turned under and butted together. Stitch the rickrack in place all around the edges of the napkin.

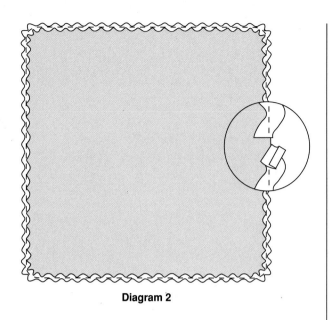

Diagram 2

2 Assembling the napkin ring

With right sides together, fold one bias strip in half lengthwise. Cut the strip to measure 19″ (48.5cm) long, as shown in **Diagram 3.** Stitch ½″ (1.3cm) from the long raw edges, as shown in **Diagram 4.** Trim the seam allowances to ¼″ (6mm) and press them open. Turn the tube right side out.

Cut one 18″ (45.5cm) length of piping cord and one 10″ (25.5cm) length of string. Referring to **Diagram 5,** wrap one end of the string several times around one end of the cord and tie tightly. Tie the other end of the string to the bottom of the safety pin. Wrap the cord end with masking tape, additionally securing the string.

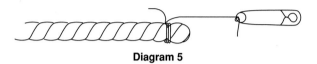

Diagram 5

Insert the safety pin into the fabric tube. Pull the string through the tube, pulling the cord into the tube until the ends of the cord are ½″ (1.3cm) from the ends of the tube. Remove the masking tape and cut off the string.

Working on one end of the tube, fold the raw ends in ¼″ (6mm), as shown in **Diagram 6.** Slip stitch the folded ends together, following the directions on page 124 for slip stitching. Repeat for the other end of the tube.

Diagram 6

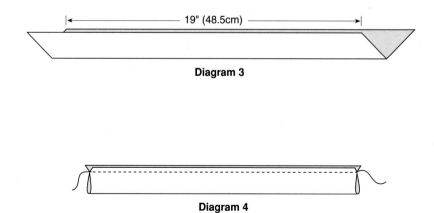

Diagram 3

Diagram 4

INSTALLATION

Referring to the photograph on page 108, fold one napkin in half and then in quarters. Accordion pleat the napkin. Wrap a tube around the center of the napkin and tie the ends in a half-knot. Repeat for the remaining napkins and tubes.

⊕ DESIGN PLUS

For elegant entertaining, create napkins and napkin rings that will truly sparkle. For the napkins, choose metallic gold rickrack and a solid or print fabric with metallic gold accents. Napkin rings fashioned from gold lamé fabric add shimmer and shine.

Celebrate in style with fast and festive touches for your holiday table.

A LITTLE BIT OF CHRISTMAS

NO-SEW PLACE MATS

Size:

Four 17½″ × 24″ (44.5cm × 61cm) place mats

SUPPLIES

- *3½ yards (3.3m) of 45″ (115cm) wide cotton or cotton/polyester fabric*
- *1¾ yards (1.7m) of 45″ (115cm) wide fusible fleece*
- *3 yards (2.8m) of 18″ (45.5cm) wide paper-backed fusible web*
- *8 yards (7.4m) of ½″ (1.3cm) wide medallion lace trim*
- *2 yards (1.9m) of ½″ (12mm) wide ribbon*
- *Fabric glue, such as Aleene's OK to Wash It*
- *Tracing paper*
- *Soft lead pencil*

CUTTING DIRECTIONS

Before cutting, review the information on page 123 for preshrinking fabric and trim.

Using the tracing paper and pencil, trace **Diagram 1** on page 114 twice, first using the solid line and the broken line for tracing the place mat pattern and then using the dotted line and the broken line for tracing the batting pattern.

Photocopy the traced patterns, enlarging them as indicated.

Trace the enlarged place mat pattern onto the paper side of the fusible web. Repeat three more times. Cut out each shape, leaving an approximately 1″ (2.5cm) margin all around. Fuse the shapes to the wrong side of the fabric, following the fusible web manufacturer's directions, and then cut out the place mat fronts. Do not remove the paper backing.

From the remaining fabric and using the enlarged place mat pattern, cut four place mat backs.

From the fusible fleece and using the enlarged batting pattern, cut four batting sections.

From the ribbon, cut four 18″ (45.5cm) lengths.

SEW SIMPLE

Small, packaged bows save you the time and bother of tying them yourself.

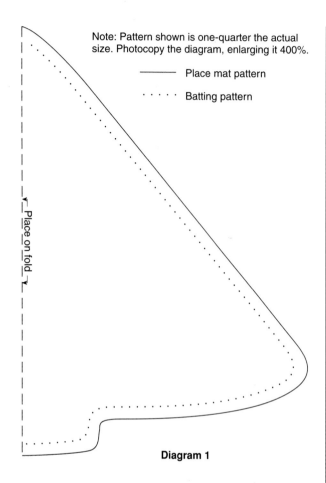

Note: Pattern shown is one-quarter the actual size. Photocopy the diagram, enlarging it 400%.

——— Place mat pattern

· · · · · Batting pattern

Place on fold

Diagram 1

FUSING DIRECTIONS

Follow these directions for each place mat.

1 Assembling the place mat

Center one batting section on the wrong side of one place mat back, as shown in **Diagram 2.** Fuse, following the fusible fleece manufacturer's directions.

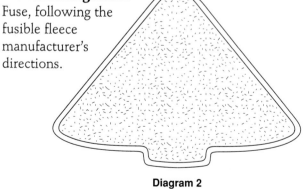

Diagram 2

Remove the paper backing from one place mat front. Referring to **Diagram 3,** with wrong sides together and raw edges even, fuse the place mat front to the place mat back, following the fusible web manufacturer's directions. Trim off ⅛″ (3mm) all around the place mat.

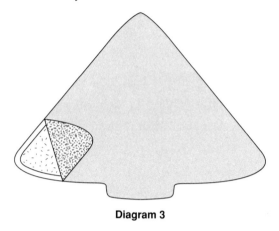

Diagram 3

2 Applying the trim

Working on the place mat back, glue the medallion lace around the edge of the place mat, positioning the lace so that the medallions extend over the edge, as shown in **Diagram 4** and in the photograph on page 112.

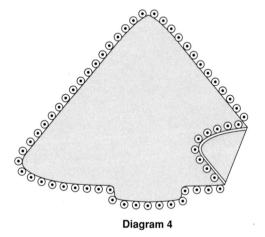

Diagram 4

Tie one ribbon length into a bow, following the directions on page 128 for tying a bow. Glue it to the place mat front, as shown in the photograph on page 112.

NO-SEW NAPKINS

Size:

Six 15″ (38cm) square napkins

SUPPLIES

- *1³⁄₈ yards (1.3m) of 45″ (115cm) wide cotton or cotton/polyester fabric*

- *11 yards (10.2m) of ½″ (1.3cm) wide medallion lace trim*

- *10³⁄₄ yards (9.9m) of ³⁄₈″ (1cm) wide strips of iron-on adhesive, such as Heat n Bond, or paper-backed fusible web, such as Pellon Wonder-Under*

- *Fabric glue, such as Aleene's OK to Wash It*

CUTTING DIRECTIONS

Before cutting, review the information on page 123 for preshrinking fabric and trim.

From the fabric, cut six 16″ (40.5cm) square napkins.

FUSING DIRECTIONS

Follow these directions for each napkin.

1 Hemming the napkin

Referring to **Diagram 1** and working on the wrong side of one napkin, apply strips of iron-on adhesive or fusible web to two opposite edges, following the iron-on adhesive or fusible web manufacturer's directions. Press the edges under ½″ (1.3cm). Let

the fabric cool; then remove the paper backing. Fold the edges back down and fuse, following the iron-on adhesive or fusible web manufacturer's directions.

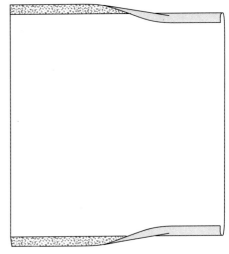

Diagram 1

Repeat for the remaining opposite edges, as shown in **Diagram 2.**

Diagram 2

2 Applying the trim

Working on the wrong side of the napkin, glue the medallion lace around the edge of the napkin, positioning the lace so that the medallions extend over the edge, as shown in **Diagram 3** and in the photograph on page 112.

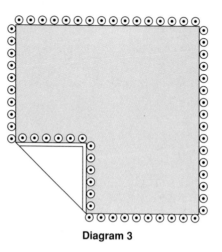

Diagram 3

NO-SEW BASKET COVER

Size:

To fit any size serving basket

SUPPLIES

- *Serving basket*
- *45" (115cm) wide cotton or cotton/polyester fabric**
- *Jumbo rickrack**
- *2 yards (1.9m) of ½" (12mm) wide ribbon*
- *18" (45.5cm) wide paper-backed fusible web**
- *Tape measure*
- *Straight-edge ruler*
- *Brown paper**
- *Soft lead pencil*
- *Fabric glue, such as Aleene's OK to Wash It*

*See the "Cutting Directions" for additional information.

CUTTING DIRECTIONS

Using the tape measure, measure the height, width, and length of the basket, as shown in **Diagram 1**.

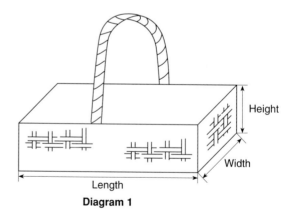

Diagram 1

Referring to **Diagram 2** on page 117 and using the ruler and pencil, draw a rectangle equal to the length and width of the basket at the center of a

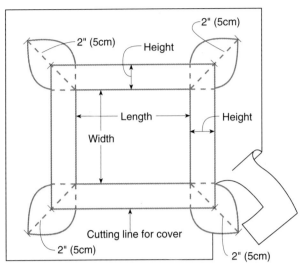

Diagram 2

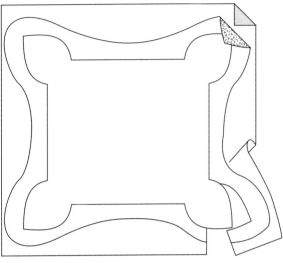

Diagram 3

large piece of brown paper. Measure out from the rectangle a distance equal to the height of the basket and mark all around, drawing another rectangle. Extend the lines of the inside rectangle to meet the outside rectangle. Draw a diagonal line that extends 2″ (5cm) beyond one corner; repeat for the other three corners. Draw a curved line on each side of each diagonal line that extends from the tip of the diagonal line to where an extended line of the inside rectangle meets the outside rectangle. Cut out the basket cover pattern.

Purchase enough fabric to cut two basket cover shapes. Purchase enough paper-backed fusible web to cut one basket cover shape.

Measure around the outer edge of the pattern. Purchase enough jumbo rickrack to equal two times this measurement plus 4″ (10cm).

Trace the paper pattern onto the paper side of the fusible web. Cut out the shape, leaving an approximately 1″ (2.5cm) margin all around.

Referring to **Diagram 3,** fuse the shape to the wrong side of the fabric, following the fusible web manufacturer's directions. Cut out the basket cover front.

Remove the paper backing and fuse the basket cover front to the wrong side of the remaining fabric, following the fusible web manufacturer's directions. Cut out the basket cover, trimming ⅛″ (3mm) from the edges of the cover front, as shown in **Diagram 4.**

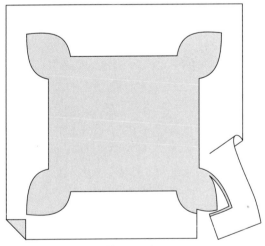

Diagram 4

GLUING DIRECTIONS

Cut the rickrack in half lengthwise. Referring to **Diagram 5** and using the fabric glue, glue one length of rickrack in place around the edge of the cover front so that the outside scallops extend beyond the edge of the cover and the cut ends of the rickrack are turned under and butted together. Glue the other length of rickrack to the cover back, matching and gluing the extending scallops together.

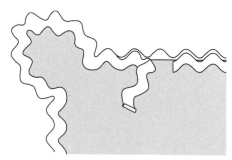

Diagram 5

INSTALLATION

Cut the ribbon into four equal lengths. Insert one length of ribbon through an opening in the basket weave at one upper corner of the basket. Adjust the ribbon until the tails are even. Repeat for the other corners.

Center the basket on the cover. Gather up one corner of the cover and secure it to the basket by tying the ribbon around it in a bow on the outside of the basket, as shown in the photograph on page 112 and following the directions on page 128 for tying a bow. Repeat for the other corners.

> ⊕ **DESIGN PLUS**
>
> *Substitute double-fold bias tape for the rickrack trim. Apply the bias tape, following the directions on page 125 for applying double-fold bias tape.*

NO-SEW STOOL COVER

Size:

To fit a stool with a 13″ (33cm) diameter seat

SUPPLIES

- *1½ yards (1.4m) of 45″ (115cm) wide cotton or cotton/polyester print fabric*
- *⅜ yard (0.4m) of 45″ (115cm) wide fusible fleece*
- *½ yard (0.5m) of 18″ (45.5cm) wide paper-backed fusible web*
- *3 yards (2.8m) of extra-wide double-fold bias tape*
- *4 tasseled chair ties*
- *Soft lead pencil*

CUTTING DIRECTIONS

Before cutting, review the information on page 123 for preshrinking fabric and trim.

From the fabric, cut:

- *One 25″ (63.5cm) square cover front*
- *One 25″ (63.5cm) square cover back*

Turn the stool upside down and center it on the adhesive side of the fusible fleece. Using the pencil, trace around the seat. Remove the stool. Cut out the batting section. Repeat, cutting out a circle of paper-backed fusible web. Do not remove the paper backing.

From the remaining fusible web, cut seventeen ¼″ × 18″ (6mm × 45.5cm) strips. Do not remove the paper backing.

FUSING DIRECTIONS

1 Assembling the cover

Referring to **Diagram 1,** center the batting section on the wrong side of the cover back and fuse, following the fusible fleece manufacturer's directions.

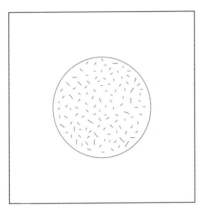

Diagram 1

Referring to **Diagram 2,** apply the circle of fusible web to the batting and apply ¼″ (6mm) wide strips of fusible web around the edges of the cover back, following the fusible web manufacturer's directions. Remove the paper backings.

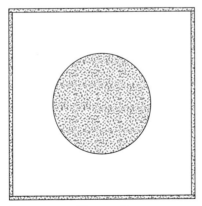

Diagram 2

With wrong sides together and raw edges even, center the cover front over the cover back. Fuse the layers together, following the fusible web manufacturer's directions.

2 Applying the bias tape

Open out the center fold of the bias tape. Working on the wrong side of the tape, apply ¼″ (6mm) wide strips of fusible web to each long edge of the tape, as shown in **Diagram 3,** following the fusible web manufacturer's directions. Be careful not to press out the center fold. Remove the paper backing and refold the tape. Apply the bias tape to the edges of the cover, following the directions on page 125 for applying double-fold bias tape.

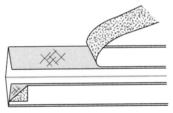

Diagram 3

INSTALLATION

Referring to the photograph on page 112, center the cover right side up on the top of the stool so that the corners of the cover are aligned with the legs of the stool. Gather up one corner of the fabric. Wrap one chair tie around the gathered fabric and the corresponding leg and tie it in a bow on the outside of the stool, following the directions on page 128 for tying a bow. Repeat, using the remaining chair ties to secure the other corners of the cover.

✦ DESIGN PLUS

Use the motifs from a contrasting print fabric to create a large appliqué for the center of the stool cover and smaller appliqués at the corners. Use paper-backed fusible web to apply the shapes, following the fusible web manufacturer's directions.

A *place mat with a pouch is perfect for picnics
and other casual dining.*

COUNTRY TIME

SUPPLIES

- *1½ yards (1.4m) of 45″ (115cm) wide cotton or cotton/polyester striped fabric*
- *½ yard (0.5m) of 45″ (115cm) wide cotton or cotton/polyester plaid fabric*
- *⅜ yard (0.4m) of 45″ (115cm) wide cotton or cotton/polyester print fabric*
- *1½ yards (1.4m) of 45″ (115cm) wide fusible fleece*

CUTTING DIRECTIONS

All measurements include ½″ (1.3cm) seam allowances.

Before cutting, review the information on page 123 for preshrinking fabric and trim.

From the striped fabric, cut:

- *Four 12″ × 18″ (30.5cm × 45.5cm) place mat fronts*
- *Four 12″ × 18″ (30.5cm × 45.5cm) place mat backs*

From the plaid fabric, cut 8 yards (7.4m) of 2″ (5cm) wide bias strips, following the directions on page 125 for making continuous bias strips. Cut the bias strip into four 67″ (171cm) lengths.

From the print fabric, cut eight 6¼″ (16cm) square pocket sections.

From the fusible fleece, cut eight 12″ × 18″ (30.5cm × 45.5cm) batting sections.

SEWING DIRECTIONS

Follow these directions for each place mat.

1 Preparing the place mat

Fuse one batting section to the wrong side of one place mat front and one batting section to the wrong side of one place mat back, following the fusible fleece manufacturer's directions.

With wrong sides together, pin the place mat front to the place mat back. Machine baste ⅜″ (1cm) from the raw edges, as shown in **Diagram 1.**

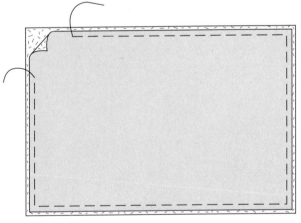

Diagram 1

⊕ DESIGN PLUS

For a country-and-western look, use denim for the pocket and the place mat and gingham or a bandanna print for the binding. Add some contrasting decorative stitching to the pocket before applying it to the place mat. For inspiration, check out the back pocket of your favorite jeans.

2 Applying the binding

Make double-fold bias tape from one 67″ (171cm) long bias strip, following the directions on page 125 for making double-fold bias tape. Apply the tape to the edges of the place mat, as shown in the photograph on page 120 and following the directions on page 125 for applying double-fold bias tape.

3 Applying the pocket

With right sides together, stitch two pocket sections together, leaving an opening along the bottom edge that is large enough for turning, as shown in **Diagram 2**. Trim the seam allowances to ¼″ (6mm) and trim the corners on the diagonal. Turn the pocket right side out and press it flat.

Diagram 2

Referring to the photograph on page 120, pin the pocket to the front of the place mat so that the lower edge of the pocket is 1″ (2.5cm) from the lower edge of the place mat, and the left edge of the pocket is 1″ (2.5cm) from the left edge of the place mat. Stitch along the side and lower edges of the pocket, through all of the layers.

✪ DESIGN PLUS

To make napkins to complement your place mats, follow the directions on page 62 for the napkins.

TERMS & TECHNIQUES

CUSTOMIZING A TABLECLOTH

The Petticoat Skirt on page 15, All Wrapped Up on page 19, Victorian Swag on page 25, and Fast Fused Flowers on page 29 can be adjusted for larger or smaller tables.

Referring to **Diagram 1,** measure the diameter of the tabletop and the height from the edge of the table to the floor. Compare these measurements to those listed in the project directions. Add or subtract the difference from the project's cutting dimensions.

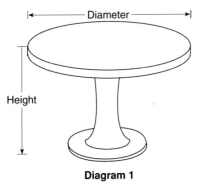

Diagram 1

When the project directions call for folding the fabric in quarters and marking a quarter-circle, as shown in **Diagram 2,** use half the diameter of the tabletop plus the height as the radius measurement.

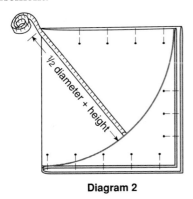

Diagram 2

PRESHRINKING FABRIC & TRIM

It is no accident that decorator fabrics are not recommended for most of the projects in this book. Decorator fabrics are treated with special finishes that are not designed to withstand frequent washings.

For tablecloths, napkins, place mats, and anything else that will be washed frequently, cotton or cotton/polyester fabrics are recommended. Washable linen can also be used. It is important to preshrink these fabrics before cutting out the project, following each fabric manufacturer's recommendations for water temperature and drying cycle. Even fabrics marked "preshrunk" should receive this treatment.

Trims, including purchased bias tape, rickrack, and lace, should be preshrunk, too, unless their fiber content is 100 percent polyester. If the trim is prepackaged and wound around a piece of cardboard, remove the wrappings. If the trim was purchased by the yard (meter), wrap it lengthwise around a 4″ × 6″ (10cm × 15cm) piece of cardboard. Bend the cardboard slightly and immerse it in hot water, as shown in **Diagram 3.** Leave the trim in the water until it cools. Remove the trim from the water and let it dry on the bent cardboard.

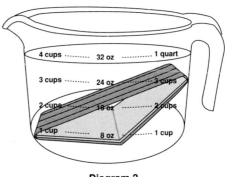

Diagram 3

SLIP STITCHING

Slip stitching provides a neat, almost invisible way to secure two turned-under edges together by hand.

To begin, knot the end of the thread. Bury the knot in the fold of the fabric. Working from right to left and referring to **Diagram 4,** pick up a single fabric thread just below the folded edge. Insert the needle into the fold directly above the first stitch and bring it out ¼″ (6mm) away. Pick up another single thread in the project directly below the point where the needle just emerged.

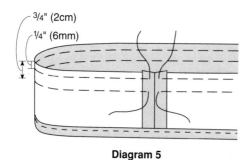

Diagram 4

RUFFLES

PREPARING A RUFFLE

Loosen the needle thread slightly. Machine baste along the raw edge of the ruffle, using two rows of stitches. Place the rows ¼″ (6mm) and ¾″ (2cm) from the edge and leave long thread tails at the beginning and end of the stitches, as shown in **Diagram 5.** Divide and mark the upper edge of the ruffle and the corresponding edge of the project into equal parts, according to the project's directions.

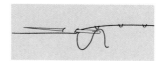

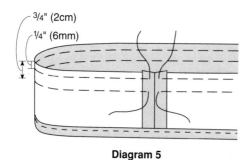

Diagram 5

GATHERING & ATTACHING A RUFFLE

Pin the ruffle to the edge of the project, matching the markings.

Pull on the bobbin thread, drawing up the basting stitches. Gather the ruffle until it fits. Adjust the gathers so that they are evenly distributed between the markings. Stitch the ruffle to the project, placing the stitches ½″ (1.3cm) from the raw edge of the ruffle, as shown in **Diagram 6.** Remove the basting stitches.

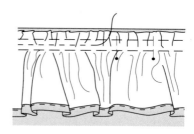

Diagram 6

BIAS TAPE

JOINING BIAS STRIPS

To join two individual bias strips, fold up one end of each strip ¼″ (6mm) and finger press. Referring to **Diagram 7,** with right sides together, pin the ends of the strips together so that the creases match and the strips form a right angle. Stitch along the crease line. Press the seam open and trim away the points that extend beyond the edge of the bias strips.

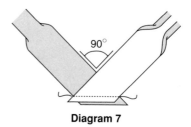

Diagram 7

MAKING CONTINUOUS BIAS STRIPS

Cut a rectangle of fabric. Trim each side of the rectangle to exactly follow a thread of the fabric. Fold down one corner of the rectangle until the lengthwise and crosswise edges meet, as shown in **Diagram 8.** Press along the fold; open out the fabric.

Cut a cardboard strip equal to the width of bias needed for your project. Using this cardboard as a template and beginning at the fold, mark parallel lines with a pencil on the wrong side of the fabric, as shown in **Diagram 9.** Stop marking when you reach a corner. Cut off the two triangles of unmarked fabric, as shown in **Diagram 10.**

Referring to **Diagram 11,** fold the fabric, with right sides together, into a tube. Match the pencil lines so that one width of binding extends beyond the edge on each side. Stitch a ¼″ (6mm) seam. Press the seam open. Starting at one end, cut along the marked line, continuing around the tube until there is one continuous strip.

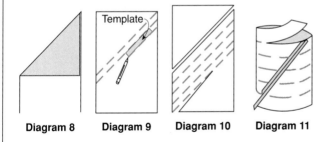

Diagram 8   Diagram 9   Diagram 10   Diagram 11

MAKING SINGLE-FOLD BIAS TAPE

To make single-fold bias tape from a continuous bias strip, place the bias strip wrong side up on an ironing board. Referring to **Diagram 12,** fold one long edge under an amount equal to one-quarter of the original width of the strip; press. Fold the other long edge under so that the long, raw edges almost meet at the center of the strip; press.

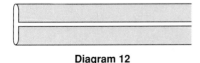

Diagram 12

MAKING DOUBLE-FOLD BIAS TAPE

To make double-fold bias tape, follow the directions for making single-fold bias tape. Then fold the single-fold bias tape lengthwise so that one long edge extends slightly below the other, as shown in **Diagram 13;** press.

Diagram 13

APPLYING DOUBLE-FOLD BIAS TAPE

Encase the raw edge of the project in the double-fold bias tape, positioning the wider side of the tape on the wrong side of the project. Pin, securing all of the layers. On the right side of the project, stitch along the edge of the tape, through all of the layers, as shown in **Diagram 14.**

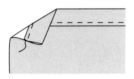

Diagram 14

To apply the tape at a corner, encase one edge all the way to the intersecting raw edge of the project, as shown in **Diagram 15.** Fold the tape down, encasing the intersecting raw edge, and pin in place, as shown in **Diagram 16.** Finger press the excess tape at the corner on both sides of the project into diagonal folds. On the right side, insert the machine needle into the tape at the edge of the fold. Stitch along the edge, through all layers.

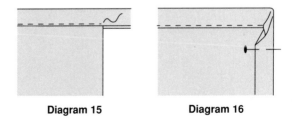

Diagram 15   Diagram 16

PIPING

MAKING PIPING

Cut and join bias strips of fabric, following the directions in "Making Continuous Bias Strips." The width of the bias strips will depend on the diameter of the piping cord. For piping cord that is up to ¼" (6mm) in diameter, cut 1½" (3.8cm) wide bias strips. For thicker piping cord, measure the cord's circumference and then add 1" (2.5cm) for seam allowances.

To cover the cord, wrap the bias strip, wrong sides together, around the cord so that the raw edges are even. Using the sewing machine zipper foot attachment, machine baste just next to the cord, as shown in **Diagram 17**. Do not crowd the stitches against the cord or stretch the bias as you stitch.

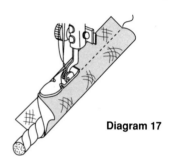

Diagram 17

APPLYING PIPING

Referring to **Diagram 18,** position the piping along the seam line on the right side of the fabric so that the raw edges are within the seam allowance and the piping cover's basting stitches are just inside the seam line. Using the sewing machine zipper foot attachment, machine baste the piping in place, stitching over the first row of basting stitches.

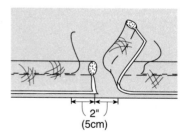

2"
(5cm)

Diagram 18

To join the ends, plan the joining to fall at an inconspicuous place on the project. Use a fabric marking pen to lightly mark the joining point.

- *Referring to **Diagram 18**, match the first end of the piping to the mark. Baste the piping in place, beginning 2" (5cm) from the mark. Baste around the project. Stop stitching 2" (5cm) before the mark, leaving the needle in the fabric and the presser foot down.*

- *Trim the piping so that the end will overlap the mark 1" (2.5cm). Remove 1½" (3.8cm) of basting stitches from the overlap. Pull the piping cover back. Trim the filler cord so that it will butt up against the other end of the cord at the mark, as shown in **Diagram 19**. Turn the end of the piping cover under ½" (1.3cm). Wrap it around the exposed cord and the beginning of the piping. Finish basting the piping in place, as shown in **Diagram 20**.*

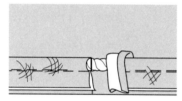

Diagram 19

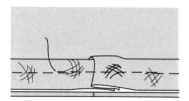

Diagram 20

To stitch a piped seam, position the project so that the section with the piping is on top. Stitch the seam, crowding the zipper foot up next to the piping so that all of the previous basting stitches will be concealed in the seam allowance, as shown in **Diagram 21.**

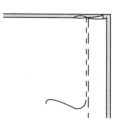

Diagram 21

NO-SEW TECHNIQUES

NO-SEW SEAMING

Cut strips of paper-backed fusible web, such as Pellon Wonder-Under, equal to the width of the seam allowance. Referring to **Diagram 22,** press one seam allowance under along the seam line. Apply strips of fusible web to the right side of the seam allowance, following the fusible web manufacturer's directions. Remove the paper backing. Lap the pressed seam allowance over the corresponding unpressed one, matching the seam lines. Fuse, following the fusible web manufacturer's directions.

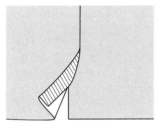

Diagram 22

NO-SEW HEMMING

On the wrong side of the fabric, apply a strip of paper-backed fusible web, such as Pellon Wonder-Under, ⅜″ (1cm) from the raw edge, as shown in **Diagram 23.** Press the fabric up along the outer edge of the paper. Fold the fabric up so that the first fold just covers the paper. Press, creasing the paper. Open out the folds. Peel off the paper. Refold the fabric and press lightly. Fuse, following the fusible web manufacturer's directions.

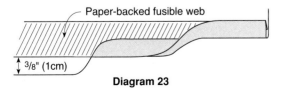

Paper-backed fusible web

⅜″ (1cm)

Diagram 23

To eliminate bulk at a point, first fuse the upper and lower edges of the panel. Apply the paper-backed fusible web to the side edges as directed above. Before removing the paper, open out the first fold. Trim the extending side hem allowance to match the intersecting upper or lower edge of the panel, as shown in **Diagram 24.** Peel off the paper, refold the fabric, press lightly, and fuse, following the fusible web manufacturer's directions.

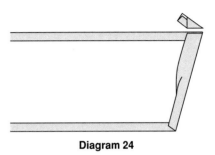

Diagram 24

STENCILING

PREPARING A STENCIL

Place the printed design over your stencil acetate with a piece of graphite paper in between. Trace the design with a pencil.

Use a craft knife to cut out the design, carefully following the traced lines. To keep a sharp edge and prevent the stencil from tearing, change the knife blade often.

It may be necessary to reverse the design to get a mirror image. To do this, either make a second stencil, reversing the direction of the design, or turn the same stencil over and use the other side. For the latter, stencil the first side of the design. Wipe off the excess paint. Spray with a fixative, such as Krylon, to seal the paint, following the fixative manufacturer's directions. Let the stencil dry for at least 15 minutes; then turn it over and stencil the design in reverse.

APPLYING STENCIL PAINT

Some designs work better if you start stenciling at the center and work out to the edges.

Hold the stencil brush straight up. Use a dabbing or circular motion to get the paint out of the container and onto the brush.

Position the stencil on the fabric. Using the same circular motion with the brush, apply the paint to the stencil, as shown in **Diagram 25**. Because it takes very little paint to fill in the stencil, it is better to apply a few light layers of paint rather than one heavy one.

Diagram 25

Test the stencil on a scrap of the actual fabric before stenciling your project. If not enough paint is getting through, slightly enlarge the stencil opening. Be careful. Enlarging it too much may weaken the stencil.

A torn stencil can be temporarily patched with Scotch Magic tape. Place a piece of tape over the tear on both sides of the stencil. If the tape overlaps into the stencil openings, use the craft knife to recut the design.

To apply more than one color of paint to a design, use Scotch Magic tape to cover the stencil openings that are not for the paint color you are using.

Oiled stencil paper can be used in place of stencil acetate. However, it requires some additional handling techniques.

- *Trace the design onto the rough side of the paper.*

- *If the stencil will be used several times, varnish or shellac the paper after the design has been cut out. This will help make the stencil sturdier.*

- *Position the stencil rough side down on the fabric.*

TYING A BOW

Referring to **Diagrams 26** and **27,** fold the ribbon or bow section in half lengthwise. Tie a half-knot at the center.

Fold the bottom end to one side and back over on itself, forming a loop, as shown in **Diagram 28.**

Bring the other end over the loop, and then under and up between the loop and the half-knot, as shown in **Diagram 29,** to form the knot and the second loop at the same time.

Pull both loops tight until they are an even size and the ends are an even length, as shown in **Diagram 30.**

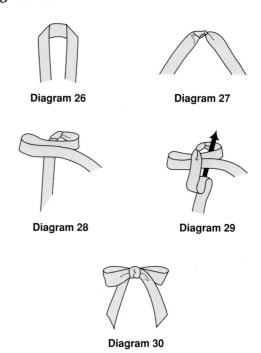

Diagram 26　　　　**Diagram 27**

Diagram 28　　　　**Diagram 29**

Diagram 30